Eleanor

CW01498884

The fascinating true story of high medieval Europe's most infamous duchess and queen.

By Laurel A. Rockefeller

Cover art derived from the Codex Manesse, 1304

Eleanor of Aquitaine

This book is a work of narrative history based on events in the life of Eleanor of Aquitaine (Aliénor d'Aquitaine) and constructed using primary and secondary historical sources, commentary, and research.

Consulted sources appear at the end of this book. Interpretation of source material is at the author's discretion and utilized within the scope of the author's imagination, including names, events, and historical details.

ISBN: 9798833056448

©2022 by Laurel A. Rockefeller

All rights reserved.

Laurel A. Rockefeller

Check out these related Biographies by Laurel A. Rockefeller

Margaret of Wessex: Mother, Saint, and Queen of Scots

Gwenllian ferch Gruffydd, the Warrior Princess of Deheubarth

Empress Matilda of England

Hildegard von Bingen

Share your love of this book and the Legendary Women of World History Series by kindly reviewing this book on your blog, website, and on major retailer websites. Your review not only offers this author your feedback for improvement of this book series, but helps other people find this book so they can enjoy it as well. Only a few sentences and a few minutes of your time is all it takes to share the love with those who want to enjoy it too.

Eleanor of Aquitaine

Table of Contents

Laurel A. Rockefeller
Eleanor, Fairest Eleanor

Tell me tales of romance and chivalry!

Beautiful ladies in elegant castles

Wooed by knights filled with courtesy and poetry!

Robin Hood fighting for justice!

For her, the troubadours did first sing!

Eleanor, fairest Eleanor!

Forever shall we sing of thee!

Tell me about the real Eleanor!

The daughter who inherited her father's wealth and lands

More than enough to make her queen of France.

Falconer. Dancer, Singer

Crusader. Lover. Queen. Mother

Ah Eleanor, we do love thee!

Eleanor of Aquitaine

More than Matilda's daughter-in-law.

More than Henry II's estranged wife

More than mother to kings of England

Eleanor, fairest Eleanor!

Forever shall we sing of thee!

Laurel A. Rockefeller
Chapter One: Duchess of Aquitaine

Sunrise broke gaily over the fields, rivers, and ponds in and around Bordeaux, Aquitaine. As servants prepared her favourite mare for riding, Eleanor listened to the many melodies of bird song around her. Pigeons and doves cooed. Song birds greeted the day with complicated tunes taught to them across the infinite ages of ancestors. Cockerels crowed to their hens to get up and start foraging for food. In the distance seabirds cried, bouncing on the winds while they hunted for fish and shellfish. While humans tried to keep to their beds, Mother Nature was feeling loud and boisterous.

"Are you sure you want to carry her yourself?" asked the Archbishop's falconer as Eleanor mounted her horse expertly.

Eleanor offered her gauntleted arm to the falconer and the beautiful peregrine he held, "I'll be fine. I hunt regularly with peregrines. This one is my favourite. Belle is her name."

The falconer handed Belle to Eleanor, "She's lovely and very well behaved. Do you want me to bring out the dogs to help flush the ducks?"

"By all means, yes. Belle knows her job. But if you have dogs to help her, that would be most appreciated."

Eleanor of Aquitaine

Eleanor, Belle, the falconer, and three of the archbishop's favourite dogs rode out to the pond where the archbishop preferred to hunt. Spotting several ducks and drakes on the pond casually enjoying their breakfast, the falconer signalled to Eleanor that he was ready to flush the game as soon as she was ready. Quietly Eleanor loosened the hood from Belle's head with her teeth before grabbing the top and removing it entirely. Belle shook out her feathers, stretched her wings, and wagged her tail, re-orienting herself to her new location. In a matter of seconds she was ready, scanning the terrain around her for prey. Eleanor nodded at the falconer to begin.

In the blink of an eye the dogs rushed at the ducks, splashing the water noisily. Belle burst off Eleanor's wrist with even faster speed, wringing to great height before choosing her prey. With eyes expertly tracking her prey's flight, Belle stooped, accelerating to over 100 miles per hour before her powerful talons struck the duck with a force that killed it instantly. Binding her talons deep into the flesh, she quickly brought her kill down to the ground. The archbishop's dogs quickly found her and pointed to where Belle was.

Eleanor pulled a sizable meal from a previous day's kill from her pouch and offered it to Belle. Belle released her fresh kill in favour of eating from Eleanor's gauntlet. Quietly the falconer picked up the fresh kill and hid it while Belle enjoyed her reward.

"That's a huge meal you are letting her have right now," observed the falconer. "She won't want to take down another bird if you let her have so much at once."

"I don't need another kill this morning," explained Eleanor as she watched Belle eat her breakfast. "Besides, she hasn't hunted since we left Poitiers and been forced to eat the mice we brought along for her. She deserves an extra-large meal this morning. This is our first opportunity to hunt since we arrived."

"I noticed Alix decided not to join us."

"Alix does not like outdoor pursuits. Then again, she has no responsibilities to the duchy as I do," remarked Eleanor. "I take much more after my father. I love falconry, hunting, and riding in addition to the more indoor and womanly pursuits taught to noble women like dancing, spinning, weaving, and needlework. My father being a wise man, I'm also very well-schooled in household management and finance so that when he or, in time, my husband, is away the family estates will not suffer for lack of a proper administrator. Men may claim superiority to women in all things, but at the end of the day when men are off to war or pilgrimage or some other errand they think beneath the abilities of women it is the woman of the house who maintains each household, great or small, so that there is always money for the essentials of life."

Eleanor of Aquitaine

"Like Belle's food for the long journey here," observed the falconer.

Eleanor picked up the now fully satisfied Belle and returned her hood to over her head, "Exactly like that."

Suddenly and unexpectedly two men on horseback, a messenger and his bodyguard, raced to them from the Cathédrale-Primatiale Saint-André de Bordeaux, the cathedral that was the heart of the Archdiocese, "My lady, come quickly!"

Eleanor waited for the men to arrive and dismount, "What news?"

"Your father is dead, my lady. A bout of dysentery or poison has killed him. On his deathbed he made King Louis VI le Gros guardian over both your person and your inheritance," answered the messenger.

"Under what terms?"

"I do not know all the details, Your Grace. Except that you have inherited your father's title, along with all of his lands and most of his money, all of it to be controlled by King Louis until he finds a suitable husband to transfer it permanently to," explained the messenger.

Eleanor carefully mounted her horse, Belle still firmly perched on her wrist. "Messages between Bordeaux and Paris will take at least two weeks. I suggest we all return to the archbishop's mansion.

There is much to do and I cannot accomplish it from here."

"News from Paris!" cried the herald as he hurried through the mansion serving as Eleanor's temporary capital in Bordeaux.

Pausing from her midday meal, Eleanor rose to greet him, "What news? Has King Louis le Gros responded at last concerning my inheritance?"

The herald bowed deeply, "Your Grace! The king has sent me to inform you that on the 12th of July you are to be wed here in Bordeaux to his son Louis le Jeune at the Cathédrale-Primatiale Saint-André. Abbot Suger is making all of the arrangements on your behalf as we speak."

"Without consulting me? On any of this? Strange indeed and perhaps the truest expression of the king's regard for me," scowled Eleanor. "What am I but land and money to him?"

"Do you object to that match, Your Grace?"

Eleanor of Aquitaine

"Depends on the terms of the match. Did he send any letters for me?"

The herald opened a leather pouch and handed her some papers, "This is what his majesty has written to you."

Eleanor accepted the papers from his hand, "Merci! I will look over these today and give you my reply tomorrow. In the meantime, please accept my hospitality and enjoy whatever food, drink, and comforts my court has to offer."

Weeks later an impressive procession of nearly 500 knights paraded over 370 miles from Paris down to Bordeaux, a display designed to impress Eleanor and convince her that her arranged marriage to the dauphin was more in her personal interest than King Louis'. It was an appeal to her vanity that Eleanor's keen and highly educated mind naturally questioned. All the same, since there were few suitable prospects in terms of both wealth and social standing and even fewer as close to her age as Prince Louis le Jeune, Eleanor found herself consenting to the match. For now.

Laurel A. Rockefeller

On the 11th of July the retinue arrived in Bordeaux, making a grand spectacle as it rode through the city and to the mansion that was Eleanor's palace in Bordeaux. Eleanor's chamberlain greeted King Louis le Gros and Prince Louis le Jeune as they arrived, "Bonjour, Votre Majesté. I am here to attend to your needs. Once you are ready, I will conduct both of you to her grace for the formal introductions."

"Where is Abbot Suger?" demanded King Louis.

"He is with the archbishop at his mansion. While he is happy to ever be at Your Majesty's service, he is not particularly fond of her grace nor she of him," explained the chamberlain.

"Why?" asked Louis le Jeune.

"Her grace is her father's daughter and not inclined towards demure placidity nor silence as proper for a woman. She has her own mind and follows her own inclinations and counsels. While you've been in Paris, she's managed to realign many of his arrangements for the wedding tomorrow towards her design and requirements. There is a certain wisdom towards giving the bride her own way on these things of course. For now, you will find her much more agreeable both during and, we hope, after the ceremony and grand celebrations."

"Disobedient child!" scowled the king. "How dare she alter my designs for her!"

Eleanor of Aquitaine

Louis le Jeune eyed his father, "I'm rather happy for her success in the matter. It makes the introductions much smoother, not to mention the ceremonial bedding required of us tomorrow night. I personally would rather find her willing in that matter rather than compelled by the law to lay there and wait for my body to do what is required of it." Louis paused, suddenly realizing what was finally becoming clear to him. To his father, Eleanor was but a means to the end of attaining wealth and land. But she was more than that. She was a woman being compelled to have sex with a stranger, simply because the law did not grant her the right to choose for herself the conditions of such intimacy. In this, they were almost the same. He too was compelled by his father's greed in the matter. Except his body could most likely be more easily convinced to do its job and seal this financial and political union the way his father wished.

"The Duchess welcomes into her court Louis le Jeune, by God's grace dauphin des Francs!" announced the herald as Prince Louis strode through the banqueting hall.

Louis le Jeune knelt before Eleanor's feet, "Êtes-vous Aliénor, duchesse d'Aquitaine?"

"Oui, je suis Aliénor," acknowledged the duchess.

Louis kissed her hand subserviently, "I have come here to marry you tomorrow—if you will have me."

"The arrangements are made, the contract ready to be signed. I will fulfil my part of the bargain," accepted Eleanor.

"Please find favour in me, ma belle et gracieuse duchesse," begged Louis.

Eleanor touched his face, "This is unexpected."

"You are your father's daughter, Your Grace. But I am not my father's son in temperament or inclinations. I am my father's second son. My older brother Philip was more like my father. He was crowned as king of the Franks and ruled alongside of our father for fifteen years. Then his horse threw him and he died almost at once. My father had me crowned as co-king of the Franks almost immediately after."

"Is this the Capetian way then? To crown the heir of the throne as co-ruler rather than wait until the power is completely his through his father's death?"

Louis met her eyes, "Yes! Though we aren't the only ones. The recently late Kaiser Heinrich V also shared power with his father, Kaiser Heinrich IV, in a similar fashion. Consider it on the job training of sorts. Best way I understand it all."

"You French have strange customs indeed!"

Eleanor of Aquitaine

"You don't consider yourself a French duchess?"

"Why should I? Your bloodline comes from Charlemagne, the great king of the Franks. But the dukes of Aquitaine are descended of the Gallo-Roman Desiderius of Aquitaine whose seat of power was Toulouse, not the Île de la Cité like the Franks."

"You have a sharp mind, Your Grace. I have never met a woman so intelligent and educated. You – awe me. I am both terrified and delighted to make your acquaintance and to be marrying you tomorrow!"

"Would you like to dine with me tonight?" offered Eleanor.

"Yes!"

The next morning Louis and Eleanor married in a ceremony so grand and lavish that Bordeaux has never seen its equal before or since with over one thousand guests and splendour to rival that of any coronation. In the middle of the whirlwind stood the shy seventeen year old Louis and the worldly fifteen year old Eleanor. As the feasting reached its fever pitch, the bride and groom found themselves led to an apartment located near Eleanor's that was specially set up for the Bedding Ceremony that completed their wedding and made them fully and legally husband and wife.

Inside the apartment they found a massive featherbed, its headboard covered in erotic images designed to both provoke the groom into completing his duties while being considered good luck for quick conception of children. Louis looked at the headboard in horror. Shaking, he crossed over to a sideboard filled with wine, mead, water, and various culinary delicacies, some of which he recognized as aphrodisiacs. Picking up a chalice he filled it, drained it swiftly, and refilled it before Eleanor could cross over to him.

Eleanor hugged him from behind, "Am I that frightening?"

"I've never – Aliénor, I don't know if I can do this right now."

"We must. Your father is just on the other side of that door, waiting for you to complete your duty."

"Aliénor, don't know what to do, do you?"

"Do I have first-hand experience in these things? Not really, no. I'm only fifteen and to be honest have found other pursuits more entertaining. Not to mention the Christian emphasis on virgin brides, especially for royals and nobility."

Louis faced her, "What do I do?"

"You can start by unlacing my bliaut and helping me out of it," suggested Eleanor.

Eleanor of Aquitaine

Louis nodded and carefully removed the outer dress, revealing some of Eleanor's figure from the remaining semi-sheer underdress. Nodding, Eleanor helped the shy Louis out of his clothes before helping him figure out how to remove the underdress, "You are beautiful, Aliénor!"

Eleanor walked Louis over to the bridal bed and laid down, pulling him closer to her, "Marry me!"

Trembling, Louis drew himself to his bride and fulfilled his duties, losing himself along the way. From outside the room, King Louis VI le Gros heard what he needed to hear. Content the duchess had succeeded in deflowering his good-for-nothing son, he headed to his own accommodations and slept off his wine.

"Your Highness, Your Grace, come quick!" yelled Eleanor's chamberlain as he banged loudly and persistently on their bedroom door.

Louis moaned, half with intoxication from last night's wine and half with intoxication with Eleanor's body as he finished another round of lovemaking. If Eleanor minded his persistence, his enthusiasm, or the frequency of his demands upon her, she offered no protest and appeared to share in her husband's needs.

Opening her eyes, Eleanor processed that her chamberlain needed a response. Gently, she extracted herself from Louis and rose from her bed, throwing on an underdress before going to the door and cracking it open, "What's wrong, my lord?"

"Your father in law is dead, Your Grace. Your husband is now king in his own right and you are queen of the Franks."

Shocked, Eleanor opened the door and allowed her chamberlain to enter. Eleanor pulled on her bliaut while turning to Louis, "Louis! Get up! We have responsibilities. Your kingdom requires us, *Votre Majesté*!" Throwing a tunic to Louis, Eleanor returned her attention to her chamberlain, "How soon are we needed at the Île de la Cité?"

"As soon as you can manage," replied the chamberlain.

"Very well then. Begin the preparations. Pack only essentials to travel in and with the lightest carriage you can muster. If my falconer can bring Belle and pack enough mice for the journey, I would like both of them to come with us. I assume my father in law has a mews in Paris?"

"He does, yes, Your Majesty."

"Majesty! That will take a while to get used to. I'm barely used to 'Your Grace.' But queen of the Franks I now am and queen I shall present myself as from the very beginning. We will do all of this in stages. Our persons first, then after we depart, prepare the rest of it and send to Paris as practical demands permit. My sister may stay anywhere she likes in Aquitaine, but I prefer she not travel to our court until our official coronation. Provide for her comfort and needs – within reason of course. If she could find herself being courted, I want to approve of any match she might consider before any money is allocated on her behalf. No need to bankrupt Aquitaine simply because I am duty-bound to live with my husband. Is all clear?"

"Yes, Your Grace – Your Majesty!"

"Excellent! I shall get my husband out of bed and we will join you shortly in the banqueting hall where we shall breakfast. Please tell me the hour is not yet Terce!"

The chamberlain smiled, "Fear not, milady! We roused you early enough – by Aquitaine standards. A churchman might find rising during Prime prayers exceedingly late, but you are no nun and your husband is no monk!"

Christmas 1137 arrived bright and beautifully. It was a wonderful day for not only celebrating the birth of Jesus Christ, but also for the coronation of the new king and queen of the Franks at Notre Dame de Reims. In a ceremony much smaller and less ornate than their July wedding, Louis officially became king of the Franks in his own right with the beautiful and red-haired Eleanor as his anointed queen consort. It was the official start to their royal lives together in their palace on the Île de la Cité. King Louis hoped his worldly bride would be happy in Paris, at least happy enough to give birth to strong sons able to inherit Aquitaine and merge it into the tiny French kingdom. He was wrong.

Eleanor of Aquitaine
Chapter Two: From Duchess to Queen

"Come dance with me, Louis!" begged Queen Eleanor as pipes and flutes, recorders, horns, harps and psalteries, bells and drums, and every manner of instrument played for their pleasure.

Louis shook his head, "I'm not feeling well. Please, darling Aliénor. Let me stay here by the fire and read my book!"

"You read too much and dance too little!" chided Eleanor. "Come! Please! They are playing a quadrille! You know how much I love to dance the quadrille!"

"No, darling! Go dance with someone else. Geoffrey Plantagenet has recently come to court. Rumour has it taking a break from his imperious wife Matilda. Imperatrix Romanorum! She still clings to her title from her first marriage to that contemptable Kaiser Heinrich V who gave both me and my father so much grief over the years!"

"Does she?" asked Eleanor, her curiosity erupting inside her like a volcano. "What else do you know about this Matilda?"

"She's engaged in a civil war with her paternal cousin, Stephen de Blois. She has the audacity to think that a female can inherit the throne of England! Can you believe that?! A woman!"

"I inherited Aquitaine."

"Aquitaine is a duchy! Not a kingdom!" scoffed Louis. "Anyway, Matilda and Stephen have both recently captured one another during this Anarchy conflict of theirs. Meanwhile the Plantagenet has stayed in Anjou or Maine most of the time where he is count. He's looking after their three young sons, Henry, Geoffrey, and William Fitzempress while Matilda is off on her fool's errand of a war."

"Interesting!" considered Eleanor. "Perhaps I should give this Plantagenet a warm welcome to our court!" Gliding away from her husband she slipped across the room. Geoffrey Plantagenet bowed. Eleanor accepted his kiss to her hand, "Bienvenue à Paris. Je suis Aliénor, reine des Francs et duchesse d'Aquitaine."

"I know! You are very beautiful, Your Majesty."

"Merci," smiled Eleanor. "My husband can't be bothered to dance with me; his book is too interesting. Care to replace him in the quadrille?"

"He won't mind?"

"I have a monk, not a husband," remarked Eleanor flippantly.

Geoffrey looked down Eleanor's bliaut lustfully, "When was the last time you … might I?"

"Dance with me!" repeated Eleanor.

Eleanor of Aquitaine

Geoffrey put his hands around her waist and kissed her, "Avec Plaisir!"

Midnight came. Quietly Eleanor crept from Geoffrey's guest bedroom to her own, her face flushed from Geoffrey's passionate lovemaking and intensity of desire that she had barely felt with Louis since their coronation celebrations. Memories of his passion filled her mind, making her dizzy. How could adultery feel so right and so good?

On the bed Louis snored, neither noticing nor caring that Eleanor had spent all evening with Geoffrey, both in public and private. Thankful for his ambivalence, she curled up on her side of the bed and went to sleep.

The next morning, Eleanor asked Louis to go hunting with her. Once more, Louis ignored her with pious excuses as to why he preferred reading, prayer, and the company of Abbot Suger over her. Disappointed but not surprised, Eleanor took Geoffrey hunting and riding instead, their successful kills celebrated in Geoffrey's bedroom, his enthusiasm as he enjoyed her body intoxicating her as no wine ever could. Oh that Louis would want her this much!

For two weeks Eleanor lived in the paradise of adultery with Geoffrey. Then, as suddenly as the affair started, she found herself watching Geoffrey mount his horse and return to his wife and sons. Falling to her knees Eleanor wept as she had never wept in her life before.

"Marie, I baptise you in the name of the Father," declared the archbishop as he poured warm water across the brow of Eleanor and Louis' week old daughter. "Marie, I baptise you in the name of the Son," he declared as he poured more water across the girl's forehead. Finally, he dipped his hand into the water a third time, "Marie, I baptise you in the name of the Holy Spirit." Dipping his finger in consecrated oil, the pastor drew the sign of the cross upon the infant's forehead, "Let us pray! Our Father Who Art in Heaven. Hallowed be thy name. Thy kingdom come. Thy will be done. In Earth as it is in Heaven. Give us this day our daily bread. And forgive us our trespasses, as we forgive them that trespass against us. And lead us not into temptation, but deliver us from evil. For thine is the kingdom, The power, and the glory, For ever and ever. Amen." The pastor lit a white candle, "Marie, receive the light of Christ. May your parents raise you in Christian enlightenment and guided by the Holy Spirit. Now and always. Amen."

"Amen," echoed Queen Eleanor with King Louis. As Louis thanked the archbishop and meandered away from mother and daughter, Eleanor found herself filled with mixed emotions. Four years had passed since Geoffrey Plantagenet broke her heart with his passions, a seduction that broke her wedding vows and changed her commitment to Louis yet, by its equally abrupt ending, left a hole in her heart and her life.

Louis was not a proper husband to her, no matter how hard he tried to please her. They were ill-matched to each other. Louis needed a quiet and demure wife happy to accept his touch only when he wished to give it. He needed someone like her sister Petronilla who was obedient to both him and the church with little ambition beyond hearth and home and children.

Laurel A. Rockefeller

This simply was not her. Eleanor was born to rule her country in her own right. She neither needed nor wanted a male overlord. For her, a husband should be a dear friend and companion, someone she could love and eagerly spend every minute with.

Fuelling her needs were the love songs of the minstrels and trouveres who frequented her court and filled her life with music. In these songs she was worshipped and adored, especially by brave knights willing to die for her. Some, hearing rumours concerning her affair with Count Geoffrey, even sang romantic fantasies exaggerating Geoffrey's devotion to her and never-ending pining to see her again and rekindle the passionate and usually erotic flame that once consumed them.

The reality of course concerning Geoffrey was very different. His sons with his wife Matilda were growing into men. Eldest son Henry was now 12 and becoming involved in his mother's war with paternal cousin Stephen for her throne in England. Henry was likely his mother's son with all the stubborn will of Matilda's father. Roaring lions of England, all three of them.

Eleanor of Aquitaine

"The king welcomes to his court, Abbot Bernard de Clairvaux!" announced the herald formally.

With barely a sound Bernard approached King Louis and Queen Eleanor on their royal dais at the end their modest throne room, a room far too austere for Eleanor's comfort and harmonious with Louis' almost monastic simplicity. Bowing, Bernard kissed the queen's hand, "Thank you for receiving me, Your Majesties!"

"The pope's envoy is always welcome," smiled Eleanor shrewdly, her brocaded bliaut and lavish jewellery contrasting with the abbot's simple vestments. "What news do you bring from His Holiness?"

Bernard pulled out a large manuscript bearing Pope Eugenius III's seal, "Pope Eugenius III has issued this bull, 'Quantum praedecessores' calling for a new crusade. I ask your majesties for permission to preach to you and the people of fair Paris concerning the pope's proposed crusade and explain His holiness' aspirations for this most holy endeavour."

"Present your arguments then. We will hear them," declared King Louis confidently.

"Tonight, if it pleases your majesties," suggested Bernard. With a nod of consent from Louis, Bernard bowed and left the royal presence.

Laurel A. Rockefeller

"I therefore commend you, take up arms for your pope and for Christendom!" implored Abbot Bernard on this, his third night preaching the merits Pope Eugenius' Second Crusade. "I am willing to lay down my life for Christ, are you?"

King Louis stepped forward to address both Bernard and the many nobles and Parisians packing the church, "I am, Your Excellency! I am willing to come on this crusade, to protect Christians in the Holy Land. But more than that, I am willing to obey the pope and lead our people to victory against the Saracens. Come with me, my people! We will go together in the name of Jesus Christ!"

Eleanor, as duchess of Aquitaine also stepped forward, "In the name of my homeland in Aquitaine, I too will join this crusade. All those who come from the west, come and follow me to victory! Let the name Aquitaine be known and feared by the Saracens and the kingdom of Jerusalem ruled under our banner!"

"There you have it, my friends! Both our King Louis and Queen Aliénor are leading the Crusade! Come with us and know your sins are forgiven, that you will spend eternity in Heaven for your sacrifices born on Crusade!" entreated Bernard enthusiastically. Cheers rang up. Gossip spread throughout first Paris and then across all of France and Aquitaine as thousands vowed to follow Louis and Eleanor to glory.

"Aliénor! You arrive at last!" greeted Raimond de Poitiers, his rich silk clothes marking him as Prince of Antioch.

Eleanor hugged her uncle happily, "We were attacked on the pass through Mount Cadmus. We barely made it through at all – no thanks to Louis. It's only by the grace of God he survived the attack by the Turks at all."

"Why? What happened?" asked Raimond with deep concern.

"Louis isn't used to traveling. He decided to camp for the night after I ordered our forces to press on until we cleared the mountain. That broke up our defence. Everyone who stayed with Louis and camped for the night was slaughtered. Louis only survived because he was dressed like a monk and managed to get up a tree and out of their reach. Or so I'm told by messengers. He won't arrive today, he's that far behind. Probably tomorrow," explained Eleanor, her rage flashing in her eyes.

Raimond led her through his mansion and sat her down at a table as servants rushed to bring food and wine, "You are tired, hungry, and in need of a soothing bath. A fresh change of clothes would no doubt help sooth you as well. Did you bring any ladies with you to assist you?"

"Yes! I don't know how many survived this fiasco, but about 300 ladies and gentlemen courtiers left with us. I'm hoping most survived. We were well supplied with all the comforts of home when we left Paris. Somewhere I should have some barrels of fine Bordeaux wine for you as a gift," offered Eleanor.

Raimond bowed politely, "Greatly appreciated! A taste of home is always welcome. It will delight my court."

"How are things in Antioch?" asked Eleanor.

"Very well! Better than in Damascus. No thanks to well-meaning idiots like your Louis. Such is the incompetence of fools like Kaiser Konrad III and other Christian noblemen that the Saracens have united under one of the most powerful and talented generals ever encountered in battle by Christians, a man named Saladin. Even the Knights Templar cannot defeat him! What's worse is that Christians have deepened animosity among the locals and made Saladin an even greater hero to them than he would have been! No disrespect to His Excellency Abbot Bernard, but this crusade has made conditions in the holy land worse for Christians, not better."

"Naturally! Now I wish I had consulted with you before agreeing to this mad affair," regretted Eleanor.

Raimond met her eyes, "This talk is not easing either your mind or your body. Come! Let's forget about it all. Eat! Drink! Listen to some music after your bath has refreshed you. My home is a comfortable one. Time to enjoy some of the hospitality I have to offer, at least until your idiot husband arrives."

"The prince welcomes into his court Louis le Jeune, by God's grace king of the Franks!" announced the herald as a dirt and blood splattered Louis stumbled into the cavernous room Raimond used as both banqueting hall and throne room.

Louis approached Raimond and bowed politely, his friar's habit contrasting sharply with the rich silks worn by both Raimond and the nearby Eleanor, "Your Highness I beg for your kind hospitality!" Looking up he glared at Eleanor, "I see you fared better than me getting here!"

Eleanor rose from her comfortable chair, "I was not stupid enough to make camp in the middle of a waiting ambush. Any idiot with eyes around him or a morsel of common sense would have known that was a bad place to rest for more than a few minutes. At minimum, you could have found the waiting Turks if you had sense enough to send a few scouts to reconnoitre the nearby area."

Louis straightened up proudly and met Raimond's eyes, "See how my wife dares address me!"

"Eleanor could become the greatest general of the entire crusade if she had mind to. Fortunately for you and the Kaiser she isn't interested in slaughtering Jews or Saracens. Seeing this land is enough; no need to conquer it or try to save your souls by shedding innocent blood," remarked Raimond.

"Says the prince of Antioch!" mocked Louis.

"I am prince here because I married well. I do not claim to be a military genius nor remotely an equal to Saladin," countered Raimond. Sensing the tense mood between Louis and both himself and Eleanor Raimond clapped his hands diplomatically, "Alas! Let there be no more talk of battles nor marital quarrels! Let's have food, drink, poetry, and dancing! Time for cool bathes, clean clothes, and comfortable surroundings! As I command, so it shall be!"

"What do you mean you and your Aquitaine knights are not joining our attack of Aleppo?" asked Louis, his rage boiling over at Eleanor as she contentedly drank another glass of Bordeaux wine.

"Because it's a fool's errand. Our forces are no match for Saladin's soldiers, let alone for what ambushes Saladin can devise. All of our intelligence says that Aleppo is the worst place for a Christian assault. Which is why I strongly wonder why you are so dead set on going there and sacrificing so many lives. What is the point of this?"

Eleanor of Aquitaine

"God commands –"

"Rubbish! What's the real reason, Louis?"

"I owe the pope. Penance for my sins, Aliénor. I must prove myself worthy of heaven."

"There are better ways to go about it."

"That's not for you to decide, Aliénor."

"I disagree. God never said to throw your life away, which is exactly what attacking a better equipped, better positioned, and better led defending force would be," asserted the queen.

"We are going to Aleppo. You will either come with me willingly and help us or go there as my prisoner," asserted Louis.

"You wouldn't dare!" countered Eleanor.

King Louis was true to his word. With Eleanor fiercely opposing what she and all her generals from Aquitaine considered suicide, Louis put her under house arrest. As Eleanor predicted, the attack on Aleppo was a disaster for both Louis and Kaiser Konrad III, ending the crusade for both their forces. A few weeks later Raimond took on his own foolhardy engagement against Saladin's uncle Shirkuh at the Battle of Inab. Victoriously Shirkuh beheaded Raimond and sent his head to a friend as a trophy.

Laurel A. Rockefeller

Meanwhile the journey home for Louis and for Eleanor went no more smoothly than their time in the Holy Land. Pirates attacked the ships carrying Eleanor and Louis. Evasive maneuverers intending to prevent capture meant sailing into stormy weather that blew Eleanor's ship south of the Barbary Coast. Roger of Sicily reunited the couple, enabling them to travel together to Tusculum where the pope lived in exile following a popular uprising in Rome. There, Eleanor asked the pope for a divorce from Louis. Eugenius refused, leveraging his power instead towards reconciling Eleanor with Louis.

Willing to give their marriage one last chance, Louis came to Eleanor's bed, conceiving in her a badly wanted royal baby, hoping this time it was a boy. When Eleanor delivered a healthy daughter, Louis found himself persuaded by his court to finally give Eleanor what she wanted: a divorce.

Standing before four archbishops, Louis and Eleanor each plead to dissolve the marriage. Its terms released Eleanor – and Aquitaine – from Louis and his hated French court. She was, at very long last, duchess of her own country, without a man to command her. With both her daughters entrusted to their father, Eleanor returned to Bordeaux to seek the next adventure in her life.

Eleanor of Aquitaine

"The duchess receives into her court, Henry, Duke of Normandy and Count of Anjou and Maine," announced the herald.

Happy to be finally back in Bordeaux, Eleanor received Duke Henry enthusiastically, "Bienvenue à Bordeaux."

"Merci beaucoup, Votre Grâce. I am Henry, Count of Anjou and Maine through my father and Duke of Normandy through my mother Matilda and her father."

"How is your father?" asked Eleanor.

"He died in September. But not before telling me stories of all your many virtues, of course. He was very fond of you and always remembered you well."

Eleanor rose and stepped down from her throne, guiding Henry to a quieter space away from courtiers. Reaching a much more private space for conversation, Eleanor faced Henry, "He broke my heart. He was the first man to bed me whose touch I felt any great enthusiasm for. When he left to return home to you boys and your mother it felt a very painful hole in my heart."

"I didn't know that. I don't think he knew that. If he did, perhaps he would have asked you to come to Anjou to visit us," suggested Henry.

"What would your mother have thought?"

"My mother's first thought is, perhaps appropriately, securing her usurped birth right from King Stephen de Blois. Not simply out of personal ambition, but on behalf of both Welsh and English peoples. Stephen is a terrible king who abuses his power. There is no royal justice in England. The nearest is from the Ecclesiastical Courts which, by their very nature, undermine secular power and are easily abused. What does the pope care for the laws of England – or the Welsh kingdoms, let alone for Normandy, Anjou, Maine—"

"—or Aquitaine?" finished Eleanor.

"Yes, exactly!" affirmed Henry.

"Is it true you've been fighting in England on your mother's behalf?"

"Yes! My mother retired from personally leading our forces about five years ago now. I've been in charge of them ever since. To her credit mama personally conducted our side of the war for almost twelve years. Her kinship to the kings of Alba helped, but so did her kinder, more just treatment of others. A man seeking royal justice from her was always likely to receive a fair and balanced result. She knows Welsh common law and has no inhibition about applying its better provisions towards all who call her queen. Whatever a person's politics towards women inheriting from their fathers, especially lands and titles, she has been the most just of all Angevins."

Eleanor of Aquitaine

"Without being from Aquitaine!" noted Eleanor.

"Incredible, isn't it that a 'mere' English woman could accomplish so much and be such a role model to us all. Though to be fair she spent most of her youth in Kaiser Heinrich V's courts, living with him until she was old enough to marry him," remarked Henry flippantly. "Even now she speaks better German than English. The recent death of her stepmother, Adelheid van Leuven has been a great loss to her. Adelheid was her subject when she was Kaiserin and her friend after her beloved Heinrich died of cancer and was recalled by my grandfather to England and then to marriage with my father. German was an important bond between them. Mama never gave it up. I think even after these many long years she still loves her Heinrich."

"True love! Minstrels and Trouveres sing all about love, yet I have never felt it, not romantic love anyway. The nearest I've ever come to love is my father's doting devotion to my education. But even then he was not particularly a warm or affectionate father."

"I understand about families. You may not know this, but my grandfather sired over 30 children. Of those, just five were with my grandmother, Princess Edith Matilda, the eldest daughter of Margaret of Wessex and King Máel Coluim mac Donnchadh of Alba. The rest of my mother's siblings were begotten on his mistresses, including Gwenllian ferch Gruffydd's sister-in-law, Princess Nest ferch Rhys. Three of her full blood siblings died very young. The other, a brother, died in the White Ship Disaster when his ship broke apart on some rocks off the coast of Normandy."

"Are you referring to Prince William Ætheling?"

"You heard of him?"

"Yes! Who hasn't?" asked Eleanor casually. "So that was your uncle?"

"A man too much like his father to be sensible and who ultimately died from too much partying aboard ship. The hazards on the channel between Normandy and Dover are well known. Only an idiot sails the channel at night with a drunken crew."

"Are all Angevins idiots then?"

"I'm not," flirted Henry. "Nor is my mother. She is the exception to the rule about women being the weaker sex who need strong men to make decisions for them."

Eleanor of Aquitaine

"As am I, Henri!" suggested Eleanor. "Strong personalities, both female and male, dominate in Aquitaine. We are a strong people and of far greater Gallic blood than you might expect. Perhaps because we are a coastal people. Neither Romans nor Franks managed to wipe out our ancient connections to this land."

"You sound rather proud of that heritage."

"I am my father's daughter," asserted Eleanor.

"As my mother is her father's daughter," echoed Henry.

"You know we could make a great time and forge a powerful alliance, you and me," flirted Eleanor. "Together you and me could make Louis le Jeune irrelevant and France a kingdom in name only with no more power than the smallest of baronies."

Henry touched her body provocatively, "You arouse me, dear lady! I am drunk with ambition from your words."

Eleanor kissed him, "Good!" Taking him by the hand, she led him away from the noisy hall.

Several minutes later Eleanor found herself purring happily under the covers of her great bed of state. After years of Louis and the occasional one-night affair born from excess drinking, the powerful competence in this Plantagenet's touch both delighted her and filled her with memory of his father. With barely a word between them Henry had set about his task effectively, almost as if schooled by his father on how to touch her and what she wanted from him.

Henry gazed into her eyes, "How long shall I stay here with you, Your Grace?"

"How long *can* you stay?"

"Depends on what you want of me. I am happy to indulge your needs and desires until all the lonely years fade from your memory and I become all you ever want and need."

"Oh that you would!" plead Eleanor.

Henry kissed her sweetly, "That is the work of a lover, Aliénor. But is that all you want of me? Are you willing to risk your money and lands without the protection of matrimony? For what if one happy night you should conceive without matrimony? What happens to Aquitaine then? Already I see myself quickening you, wanting, nay demanding kings of England out of you! Take me in matrimony and you shall not want for anything. Aliénor, beautiful Aliénor! Take me as your husband and you shall always conceive out of joy and pleasure, never duty! I swear it!"

Eleanor of Aquitaine

"You will have to make that declaration in public, you know. That way the necessary paperwork and contracts can be drafted."

"Naturally. But may I have your answer now?"

Eleanor touched him provocatively, "Your wife I shall be … if tonight you continue to prove yourself the powerful match I hope you are."

Dawn arrived quicker than expected. As roosters called to their hens, Henry held Eleanor with the wide awake awareness of the bargain he made. The duchy of Aquitaine would be his. All he had to do was marry her and continue to please her in bed, keeping his debaucheries with lesser women discrete and away from her notice. Wondering what Thomas Becket was doing with his time, Henry slipped out of Eleanor's bed in search of the privy, a bath, and clean clothes.

"I, Aliénor, duchesse d'Aquitaine, take thee, Henri Plantagenet, duc de Normandie et comte d'Anjou et du Maine, to be my wedded husband. I promise to be faithful to you in good times and in bad, in sickness and in health, to love you and to honour you all the days of my life," vowed Eleanor as she faced her chosen bridegroom.

"I, Henri Plantagenet, duc de Normandie et comte d'Anjou et du Maine take thee Aliénor, duchesse d'Aquitaine, to be my wedded wife. I promise to be faithful to you in good times and in bad, in sickness and in health, to love you and to honour you all the days of my life," vowed Henry. Solemnly he placed a jewelled ring on Eleanor's finger on her left hand. "With this ring, I thee wed. All my worldly goods, I thee endow. All that I have, I give to thee, Aliénor, duchesse d'Aquitaine ."

The presiding priest smiled, "What God has joined together, let no man tear asunder." Making the sign of the cross he prayed, "In nómine Patris et Fílii et Spíritus Sancti. Amen."

"A-men," echoed the bride, groom, and the congregation as they also made the sign of the cross.

The priest turned to Henry, "My lord Plantagenet, you may now kiss your bride!"

Eleanor of Aquitaine

With Thomas Becket at his side, Henry eagerly kissed Eleanor. Soon his trophy would be completely his, sealed during the bedding ceremony after the reception and secured once she birthed their first born son.

Quickening Eleanor did not take long. Within six months Henry secured Aquitaine for himself when she became pregnant with their first child, a son named William. With 1153 waning into autumn, Eleanor found herself nervous as she waited for the inevitable: a visit from her mother-in-law, Empress Matilda, rightful sovereign queen of England herself!

"The duchess welcomes into her court, Matilda, by God's Grace Imperatrix Romanorum and rightful queen of England!" announced the herald as Matilda confidently strode towards her son and daughter in law.

Eleanor rose from her throne, "Bienvenue à Bordeaux, belle-mère."

Matilda acknowledged her with bow of her head, "Merci beaucoup, belle-fille. I am sorry I missed the christening. How is my grandson?"

"Well! We named him William. He is a good boy. His servants attend to him most of the time. I visit when I can."

"As it should be," agreed Matilda. "Can you arrange for me to see him today or tomorrow?"

"Of course!"

"Merci beaucoup, Aliénor." Matilda turned to Henry, "As much as I would like to say the main reason for my visit is to meet and play with my grandson, I actually am here on other business. Specifically I need to talk with you in private, Henry. Concerning England."

"You've heard news from London?" asked Henry.

"I have. Is there somewhere more private where the three of us can talk?"

"My apartment," suggested Eleanor. "I have some wine ready to open that I think you will enjoy. Or would you prefer something more German? I heard it said you picked up quite a taste for German beers while you were growing up in Mainz?"

"Yes! My step-mother Adelheid van Leuven even made a habit of gifting me cases of beers from all corners of the Empire. Including ales from Mainz."

"Those ales may have been brewed in Mainz, belle-mère, but I have it on good authority the recipes came from Kent. Your father sent English brewers to Kaiser Heinrich's court to make English ales and beers for you and the Kaiser."

Eleanor of Aquitaine

"Which probably explains why the royal court was the only place in all the empire where I could find ales," mused Matilda.

"Logically," agreed Eleanor as she led the way to her apartment and opened the door. Henry located a servant and whispered commands to him regarding food and drink. Eleanor continued towards the sideboard and poured Matilda some wine into a silver chalice, "Try this! It is the finest red wine in all of Bordeaux."

Matilda sampled the wine expertly, "Interesting blend of flavours. Very different from what I am accustomed to."

"Our best wines are a blend of Cabernet Sauvignon with Merlot and sometimes other varietals as well, depending on the brewer. Our white wines tend to be a blend of Sauvignon Blanc and Sémillon. Some of the sweetest of sweet wines, actually," explained Eleanor as she refilled Matilda's drained chalice.

"What do you prefer to drink, Henry?" asked Matilda as she took another sip.

"Good English beers or maybe a local braggot!" declared Henry resolutely. "I don't have Aliénor's refinement when it comes to drink – or food for that matter."

"From what I could tell, my father your grandfather was much the same. The complex flavours of continental wines were too subtle for him. England suited him well in that regard."

"What news have you received concerning England, Mother?" asked Henry.

"An envoy from King Stephen's court came to me. He wishes me to send a representative to London to negotiate an end to the Anarchy. You are the logical choice and best capable of representing our interests," confirmed Matilda.

"How soon am I wanted there?"

"As soon as possible, particularly since you have the furthest distance to travel."

"Very well then, I shall leave tomorrow morning – assuming our staff can ready things that quickly," asserted Henry.

"Send me word once you arrive," instructed Matilda. "I want to be kept informed at all times concerning progress on the matter."

"Know that I, King Stephen, have established Henry Duke of Normandy as my successor in the kingdom and as my heir by hereditary right, and that I have granted and confirmed to him and to his heirs the kingdom of England. The duke, on account of this honour, grant and confirmation to him by me, had performed homage to me and has given me surety by oath, that he will be faithful to me and maintain my life and my honour to the best of his ability, according to the agreements discussed between us, which are contained in this charter. I have also given an oath of surety to the duke, that I shall keep his life and his honour to the best of my ability, and that I shall maintain him as my son and heir in everything possible and guard him as far as I can against all men.

"The archbishops, bishops and abbots of the kingdom of England have at my command sworn an oath of fealty to the duke. The archbishops and bishops on both sides have undertaken that if either of us departs from these agreements, they will visit him with ecclesiastical justice until he amends his errors and returns to his observance of the aforesaid compact. The duke's mother, his wife, his brother and all his men whom he can involve in this have likewise given surety.

"I shall act in the affairs of the kingdom with the duke's advice. I myself shall exercise royal justice in the whole kingdom of England, both in the duke's part and my own. I shall act in the affairs of the kingdom with the duke's advice. I myself shall exercise royal justice in the whole kingdom of England, both in the duke's part and my own," read King Stephen as Archbishop Theobald watched the king officially end with a stroke of a pen the civil war that began with Stephen's coronation almost exactly eighteen years before. Putting the pen down King Stephen embraced the twenty-year-old duke, "You are now my son and heir, Henry."

Henry embraced King Stephen dutifully, then stepped back, "Your treaty is deceptive, my liege. I was a mere two and a half years old when this war started. My quarrel with you has been on behalf of my mother. This is and was her fight for her birth right."

"Does that mean you will not sign the treaty? Must the war continue forever?" asked Stephen.

Henry picked up a pen and dipped it in ink, "The war ends now." With scratching strokes Henry signed his name, then put the pen down. "It is done. But it is not well done. I am my mother's son and proud to be of her most royal blood. I am Norman and Saxon and Scottish blood, all kingly. I through my wife Eleanor possess a realm already larger and greater than yours. My grandsire was a great man. I shall be even greater. History shall forget you except in how you cheated a great woman out of what was hers. I shall be truly immortal."

Eleanor of Aquitaine

"I am tired of war, Henry, tired of this old argument. Eighteen years is long enough. Hold your grudge if you will, but speak of it never to me again while I live. This is my command as your king!" proclaimed Stephen.

"As you wish, my lord and king," bowed Henry Plantagenet.

Christmas came to Normandy, Anjou, Maine, and Aquitaine. With the Treaty of Westminster signed and sealed, Henry Plantagenet felt triumphant as he took the long journey from London to Rouen. There, if all went according to plan, he would celebrate Christmas with his family as the glorious heir to the English throne.

After two weeks of arduous travel, Henry rode his grand stallion through the gates of the ducal castle complex. A groom met him and held the reins as he stepped down to the ground. Henry handed him a sous as gratuity. Navigating his way through the palace, Henry headed for the ducal chapel in search of his family. Eleanor fussed with the chapel's crèche, "Joyeaux Noël, Henri."

Henry rushed up to her and kissed her passionately, "Joyeaux Noël, Aliénor."

"Success in your negotiations?"

"Stephen made me his heir. Soon you shall be queen of England, ma Cherie!"

"I know … so does your mother."

"How? I didn't write to her …."

"You think the rightful queen of England and the only surviving child of King Henry of England has no resources of her own? No power at all in her kingdom? What do you think she's been doing these last eighteen years, Henri? Of all the Angevin princesses, she alone mounted her horse and led men into battle! No king can match her wit, her intelligence, or her prowess in battle. Yet what do you and Stephen agree to?"

"Nonetheless, it is I who shall rule England," asserted Henry.

"Which is exactly why I would tread carefully around your mother," advised Eleanor.

"Where *is* my mother right now?"

Eleanor of Aquitaine

"Last I saw, playing with the baby along with your brothers. We've had quite the happy Christmas so far. Please don't ruin it by bringing up the Treaty of Westminster! Not until Fête des Rois and we've all finished eating our galette des rois cakes! For the sake of family peace and harmony, Henri! I beg you!"

Henry glared at her, "Why should I have to behave myself! I outrank her now!"

"You will never outrank your mother, Henri. Get that through your stupid, obstinate head!"

"What are you not telling me, Aliénor?"

"Henri – it's Christmas. Let's not fight. Let's have a happy time together as a family. Our chefs have prepared delicious food. Let's gather together and eat and drink and celebrate. No politics!"

Henry growled uncomfortably, "Very well then. But just until Fête des Rois! Then I must speak my own mind and attend to my own affairs as all men must."

"News from London! News from London!" shouted the messenger as he swiftly navigated the ducal palace in Rouen. Sitting more or less together in a semi-private drawing room, Matilda sat on a comfortable window-sill bench, reading a book. Eleanor "fiddled" out a tune she liked on her favourite rebec. Henry and his youngest brother William Fitzempress played chess. With a sudden explosion of light from the opening of heavy wooden doors, the messenger bowed to each member of the family, "My liege! I bring news from London."

Matilda rose imperiously, "What news?"

"King Stephen de Blois died in Dover on the 25th," announced the messenger. "The throne of England has passed to a man named Henry Plantagenet, whoever he may be."

Henry rose and met the eyes of the messenger, "I am Henry Plantagenet, son of Count Geoffrey and Empress Matilda of England."

The messenger bowed very deeply, "All hail to thee, Henry King of England!" After a moment the messenger noticed his customary salute was not echoed by anyone else in the room. "Why does no one else salute our great and glorious new king?"

"My relatives salute me? I get no respect from them, no worship. I am surrounded by family who consider me no better than their equal," scowled Henry.

Eleanor of Aquitaine

Matilda put down her book and reached out to the messenger graciously, "Forgive my son. He is ill tempered as usual. He is his father's son more than mine."

The messenger kissed Matilda's hand, "It is said you learned your manners in the Kaiser's court."

"I was the last Kaiserin of the Salian dynasty if that is what you mean, good Sir!" acknowledged Matilda graciously. "Being the only survivor of King Henry and Queen Edith Matilda's five children helped, but I find royalty is a matter of leadership, not entitlement. My eldest son disagrees; hence you find the rest of us reluctant to indulge his ego. Loyalty won through kindness and justice endures far longer than loyalty won through physical prowess and military victories. Fortunately for all of us he married well. My daughter in law Aliénor is both kind and just. She will make a wonderful queen of England."

Recognizing the compliment, Eleanor put down her rebec and joined them, "Merci beaucoup, belle-mère. Tell me, kind Sir, do you have any further information for us? When are we expected in London?"

"The day of your coronation is a matter of your discretion. However, the sooner you come to London to take possession of your capital, the more confident the people will be towards the continuation of their government," explained the messenger.

"Understood," replied Eleanor. "The date of our coronation is a heavy matter for us which requires some time to ponder and decide upon. Until then, please accept our hospitality. For surely you are both tired and hungry. Take rest here among us!"

The messenger bowed, "Thank you, Your Grace. Gratefully I accept your kindness."

The church at Westminster glittered as it had not since its consecration almost exactly eighty-nine years before. Under its altar lay King Edward the Confessor who died a mere week later. For eighty-nine years the altar served as a pilgrimage site. But today Edward was all but forgotten. Today was all about the new king ascending to his throne, a man whose most recent shared ancestor with Edward the Confessor was none other than Æthelred II Unread, many generations ago.

In resplendent ceremony the archbishop of Canterbury crowned Henry as King Henry II Plantagenet and the very pregnant Duchess Eleanor as Eleanor Queen of England. Vows of service both took in response to their sombre anointing. Multiple crowns the archbishop placed on their heads, each fulfilling a different symbolism. After more than two hours the service completed and the king and queen rose from their thrones to process out of the church and into the London streets. Cheers rose up. Eighteen years of civil war seemed to melt away in the glory of their coronation service and the many parties spreading through England. The warmongering and tyrannical Angevins were gone in favour of the peaceful Plantagenet. Peace, at very long last, belonged to England and its people.

Shrewdly the queen mother Matilda watched King Henry II and Queen Eleanor enjoy the success and adoration denied her. Henry might take the credit, but in her heart Matilda understood there was more to ruling a country than jewelled crowns and pretty clothes. To keep the kingdom, Matilda and Eleanor would have to accomplish behind the scenes what her hot tempered son could not.

There was just one practical problem for this dynasty that now mutated from Angevin to Plantagenet: Eleanor was just as ambitious as Henry.

Laurel A. Rockefeller
Chapter Three: The Plantagenets

1155 dawned bright and glorious. As Fête des Rois completed the Christmas season, Eleanor waited eagerly for the labour pains she knew were coming, her first as queen of England. On the twenty-eighth of February, 1155 she gave birth to her second child, a son they christened "Henry" after his father and great grandfather. This son, this second son gave Henry great joy. With two sons Henry felt his throne secure—along with possession of Aquitaine as a permanent part of his domain.

God intervened, humbling King Henry II's great pride. While at Wallingford Castle near London, a seizure unexpectedly took William. At only two and a half years old the little prince died suddenly. It was the first of many tragedies that family would bring to the proud Henry. Pregnant again, Eleanor grieved the loss of her eldest son even while suffering through the pains and discomfort of this, her fifth child and third with Henry.

In 1156 Eleanor's stamina of both mind and body rewarded her with a healthy daughter she named Matilda after the baby's doting grandmother and well-remembered Scottish great grandmother. This grandchild Empress Matilda especially loved; her only daughter, the Prinzessin Royal and heiress to the German Salian dynasty only lived a few minutes. But this baby, this Matilda Plantagenet was strong and already born with Eleanor's good looks. Before even the girl's christening, Empress Matilda knew the girl would want for nothing. Gladly Eleanor allowed Empress Matilda a grandmother's privilege to coddle the girl as she wished. She deserved cherishing. She deserved to grow as strong and independent as she Eleanor had grown under her own father's cherishing and indulgences.

Richard came the following year in 1157. In September 1158 Eleanor gave birth to son Geoffrey. In 1161 Eleanor gave birth to her namesake daughter, Eleanor of England. In 1165, Eleanor gave birth to her final daughter, Joan of England, Finally, on Christmas Eve, 1166 she gave birth to the baby of the family: John whom King Henry II called "Lackland."

In all, two daughters by Louis le Jeune. Five sons and three daughters by King Henry II of England. Ten children altogether. It was an exhausting tenure as first queen of France, then queen of England. Drained by constant pregnancy, childbirth, and the incessant need to smooth over the many feathers ruffled by her husband's brutish personality and style of governing, Eleanor found herself unable to cope further. Staying in London just long enough for John's christening and for the Fête des Rois celebrations, Eleanor packed her most prized belongings for a prolonged stay back home.

"It's true then? You are leaving?" asked Empress Matilda as she watched Eleanor sort through the last of the trunks she wished to take across the English Channel.

"Yes!" confirmed Eleanor as she very neatly refolded a dress and gently returned it to the trunk. "Nothing against you, Belle-Mère. I've fulfilled my duties to the kingdom and, quite frankly, I just cannot endure any more of Henri's nonsense. I am worn out and need time away from him!"

"So do we all," smirked Matilda. "Especially now there's animosity between him and Thomas Becket. Henry has grown intolerable."

"Henry never expected Thomas to change from the worldly archdeacon who barely minded religion to the devout chancellor and then archbishop of Canterbury that he's become."

"Like my father and his namesake, Henry has always framed people and events in absolute terms. He is easily blinded by adoration and loyalty, often missing key cues about people, especially when they are manipulating him."

Eleanor of Aquitaine

Eleanor nodded, "It never occurred to him that when Becket took the job as archbishop of Canterbury that Becket would prioritize the demands of the job – including deference to the pope – over their long friendship. But Becket does have other values than the king. He always wants to do his work, whatever that may be, to the best of his abilities."

"The problem is that the duties and responsibilities of the archbishop of Canterbury are completely different in focus from that of the royal chancellor. For a chancellor, the priority is serving the king's interests – which Henry likes. But bishops and archbishops owe their allegiance to the pope and their duties to those in their dioceses. They operate independent of the Crown," observed Matilda.

"Something Henry absolutely hates. He does mean well, but when a priest murders, the trial is held in ecclesiastical court and without the penalty of death if he is convicted. But if the same trial is held in the king's courts, the accused is very likely to be put to death. If the penalties were consistent across both sets of courts, that would be one thing. But the extraordinary leniency the Church extends to its own when its clergy misbehaves is more than Henry can tolerate. In this, I must agree with him," confirmed Eleanor.

"Where will you go from here?" asked Matilda.

"Poitiers. My sister is meeting me there. The children, for now, will stay here with their father. I love them, but I also need some time away from them. At least for a little while," confessed Eleanor.

Matilda hugged Eleanor, "Well then, God speed you on your journey and keep you safe, Aliénor. May you find the peace you so greatly deserve."

Eleanor thrived in Poitiers. As her children grew up, mostly in England, Eleanor found herself in a better position to advance their interests and that of each region of her kingdom than she ever could living in England with Henry. She secured strategic marriage alliances for her daughters and fought to protect her sons' interests when first King Louis VII, then his son and successor King Philippe II Auguste threatened their birth rights.

Eleanor of Aquitaine

In 1168 King Henry elevated the eleven year-old Richard to duke of Aquitaine, legally depriving Eleanor of her power over her homeland. Fortunately for Eleanor – and the people of Aquitaine – Richard had no real interest in the day to day governing of Aquitaine. Or any land for that matter. Warfare and soldiering interested Richard the most, a passion suitable for a third son of a king and therefore with no real chance of needing to assume the throne after his father's passing.

As years passed, the feud between King Henry and Archbishop Thomas Becket increased in hostility. On the 1st of December, 1170 Becket returned to Canterbury. Crowds and monks alike cheered Becket's return, aggravating an already agitated Henry. In a drunken stupor, King Henry raged, "What miserable drones and traitors have I nurtured and promoted in my household who let their lord be treated with such shameful contempt by a low-born clerk!" Knights Reginald FitzUrse, William de Tracy, Hugh de Morville, and Richard le Bret overheard the king's anguish and, dutifully, took it upon themselves to alleviate the king's suffering. On the 29th of December they carried out their gruesome task, murdering Thomas Becket after several blows with their swords and wounding nearby monk Edward Grimm. The resulting shock and outrage was quickly answered by the people and by Rome when, on the 21st of February 1173 the pope canonized Thomas Becket into a saint, one of the fastest such canonizations in church history.

Meanwhile Eleanor remained in Poitiers in exile, forbidden to set foot in England except when in King Henry's company, yet in practice ruling not only Aquitaine and Poitou, but Normandy and Anjou as well. It was a strange disconnect between who was officially in charge and who was actually in charge, though few outside of the governments realized this distinction.

"Tell me, Mother, what do you think of the latest song about King Arthur?" asked Marie, Comtesse de Champagne. Now in her late twenties, Eleanor's eldest daughter had grown strong, beautiful, and a force of nature unto herself, her mother's daughter despite growing up with her father King Louis VII le Jeune.

Sitting in comfortable chairs around a roaring fire Eleanor and Marie were joined by Eleanor's favourite son Richard and by the leading noblewomen of Aquitaine, Poitou, Normandy, Anjou, and Maine in a grand salon focused on enjoying, debating, and patronizing the music, arts, and literature that Eleanor so famously indulged in and that thrived so vigorously in her court.

Standing up from his chair near his mother, Prince Richard raised his voice, "I don't know about you, Mama, but I really liked the song! Please ask the trouveres to sing it to me again when I go to bed?"

Eleanor of Aquitaine

Eleanor smiled at Richard, her son so beloved that he alone of his father's children with her could not bear to be parted from his mother when she left England, "If you like, Richard. But I think you fill your mind too much with tales of war and of battles. How can you learn to rule when you know nothing about people?"

"I know enough!" asserted Richard. "I know it was right when those knights obeyed my father and rid us all of Becket!"

Marie chided her younger half-brother, "The Pope disagrees with you about Becket, Coeur de Lion. Becket is a saint now and pilgrims flock to Canterbury to his tomb."

"The Pope hates mother. So did that Bernard de Clairvaux. Good riddance!" pouted Richard.

"Abbot Bernard did not like Mother, but he supported Abbess Hildegard von Bingen, encouraging her to listen to and write down her Visions. If not for Bernard, would Hildegard be touring the German Empire preaching and teaching what she's learned and discovered?" countered Marie.

"Marie is right," added Eleanor. "Hildegard is a model of what women are and can be. She even believes in romantic love and has some wonderful theories about sex, love, and its role in the Divine. And while I've never heard her speak myself, I have heard stories from those who were fortunate enough to attend her sermons and read her books. Fascinating if not very complex ideas!"

"Isn't there a song about Hildegard and love?" asked one of the ladies sitting nearby.

"If not, Master Trouvere, can you make one up?" asked another.

With a quiet bow the lead musician entertaining them whispered to his colleagues and soon began to play and sing.

Prince Richard did not stay long in Poitiers at his beloved mother's side. With his father continuing to play power games among his sons, teasing them with promises of power that he kept in name only, eldest surviving brother Henry the Young King had enough. Eleanor felt sympathetic and happy to lend her wisdom and talents to her boys, a series of plots emerged with most of Henry's domestic and foreign enemies. The objective: to depose King Henry and set up the Plantagenet princes as regional rulers in their own rights.

Eleanor of Aquitaine

"Is everything ready?" asked Eleanor as she finalized her preparations to leave her palace in Poitiers. Wearing a simple linen bliaut over an undyed linen kirtle and with a veil and wimple covering her hair and neck Eleanor looked more like a merchant's wife than a duchess and queen, a disguise she hoped would fool Henry's spies.

"We will leave the castle through the servants' hallways until we reach the kitchens and the final doorway out," confirmed Eleanor's head lady-in-waiting. Leading the way she and Eleanor dodged several man servants, none of them particularly trusted by Eleanor. After several minutes they reached the last door. "Wait here a moment!" Sneaking through the door, the lady waved to the queen it was safe to leave the castle. "Okay, let's make a hurried walk to the stables! If our friends have kept their word your horse should be ready."

Quickly and walking as fast as she could without breaking into an obvious run Eleanor dashed for the stables. Locating her horse she leapt upon her back as two of her ladies reached their horses and mounted them. Grateful now for the horsemanship skills learned from her passion for falconry Eleanor turned her beautiful mare towards the gate and urged her through to freedom.

Hours later Eleanor and her ladies stopped their horses for a badly needed rest. Dismounting they let their feet touch the muddy grass as the horses drank deeply from a nearby stream. Scanning the lush fields around them Eleanor watched for signs of pursuit. None that she could see. Cautiously she and her ladies mounted their mares and continued on their way to Paris.

"Your Majesty, I am here to arrest you!" barked the knight as he and about a dozen foot soldiers surrounded the small camp Eleanor and her ladies made for the night.

Slowly Eleanor opened her eyes, half expecting the shouts and noise to be from a dream and not the waking reality around her, "On what charges am I arrested?"

"Conspiracy to depose the king in favour of your son Henry," barked the knight as one of his foot soldiers shoved Eleanor up and out of her grassy bed.

"Have you proof of such conspiracy?" asked Eleanor as she found her feet and brushed her nightgown clean.

"The king needs no proof to arrest you, Madame."

Eleanor of Aquitaine

Eleanor eyed him, "The king is a boorish egotist whose vanity supersedes all other considerations. Hence the Becket matter and why the pope so swiftly beatified him."

"Nonetheless you are hereby arrested," asserted the knight.

"Not until I dress myself I am not! Now back off and allow me and my ladies some privacy while we clothe ourselves. Or would you prefer I report to the king that you arrested me still naked and without the most basic of dignities afforded to the nobility?"

Chided, the knight and his soldiers backed off several feet and turned their backs to permit Eleanor to dress.

Several days later Eleanor and her ladies in waiting found themselves in Wiltshire at a castle called Old Sarum. As a prison, it was comfortable enough. But it was still a prison. Everywhere in the castle and outdoors on the castle grounds that she went followed one of the king's most loyal servants. Everything that she did was recorded. Every word she spoke to one of

her ladies was reported about. No messages reached
her that were not first read by either the king or
someone working for the king. Unlike her exile in
Poitiers she was afforded no court, no ability to govern
anyone or anything. She was at Henry's mercy at all
times, a man she knew was readily cruel when he felt
slighted.

Across 1173 and through much of 1174 Henry
experienced enormous luck in his war with his sons. In
eighteen months, it was all over and the entire family
was forced to renew their vows of fealty to the king.
On 30th September 1174 the Revolt of 1173-1174 was
officially ended with a ceremony in Normandy. As
news reached Eleanor of Henry's victories it became
abundantly clear: as long as King Henry breathed she
would not be free of her prison.

"The king is dead! Long live the king!" heralded
messengers as they spread across England. Reaching
Old Sarum Castle, home to Eleanor during most of her
house arrest at King Henry II's hands, the messenger
sent from King Richard found Eleanor preparing for
another beautiful day riding her favourite mare and
hunting with her newest gyrfalcon. Humbly he bowed

to her, "Your Highness, I am sent to inform you that King Henry II Plantagenet is dead. Your son Richard Coeur de Lion rules England and all your possessions across the channel now."

Eleanor crossed herself with relief, "Gloria Patri, et Filio, et Spiritui Sancto. Sicut erat in principio, et nunc, et semper, et in saecula saeculorum. Amen. Merci beaucoup, kind sir! These are most glad tidings indeed!"

"King Richard bade me also tell you: your years of exile and house arrest are over. You are this day free to come and go and live as you wish."

"Where is my son the king now?"

"Rouen."

"Tell my son the king I shall come meet with him at the palace there before the end of the month. His coronation must be celebrated as the grand affair it deserves to be. I shall assist him. No man or woman must be allowed to think the king a lesser son of an overly bullish and disagreeable Angevin lord. Rather the name Richard, Coeur de Lion must ring out glorious on the tongues of all who hear it!"

Inspired by the lavish honey in the dowager queen's voice, the messenger beamed brightly, "So shall it must be, Your Highness! So shall it will be! Let the name Richard Lionheart be remembered forever!"

Eleanor arrived in Rouen just as the catholic priests began their celebrations of the first fruits of the harvest, a holiday holdover from Celtic times known in the church as Lammas or "loaf mass." Cheers rang up as she passed, many of them paid for in advance to encourage widespread love for both her and Richard. Each of these paid for cheers triggered others to cheer until to the untrained eye hundreds if not thousands of people appeared to rejoice in Eleanor's return.

Reaching the palace, Eleanor efficiently navigated her way through well-worn pathways, corridors, and stairways to the Great Hall that on most days served as both the banqueting hall and the centre of the ducal or royal court, depending on who was in residence at the time. King Richard walked swiftly through the hall to greet her, "Mother! You arrive at last!"

Eleanor hugged and kissed her son, "How are you, Richard?"

"Very happy to see you, Mother!"

Eleanor looked at him closely, "So I see. Your appearance and your court clearly needs a woman's touch."

Eleanor of Aquitaine

"I am a soldier, Mother. But the people need something more of their kings. They must respect me and my authority. I must be more than my father's third son."

"There's nothing wrong with being the third son, Richard. Your own great grandfather King Henry I of England was the fourth son of his father and the second to rule England after his older brother William II Rufus," reminded Eleanor. "Your older brothers are dead, perhaps before their time. But in dying young, the path is made for you to rule as king, just as it was for your great grandfather."

"You would think I would be prepared for all of this – but I'm not, not now it comes to it," confessed Richard.

"Would you like my help?" offered Eleanor.

"Would you? Could you please? I'm a soldier, not a courtier! But you, dear Mother, you've always kept a refined court. So many advances in music, dancing, and royal ceremony are through your influence and guidance. You have transformed the idea of royalty into a romantic one filled with fine food, arts, music, and luxurious living. Castles are no longer perceived as dark, cold fortresses but the seats of chivalrous glory. Tales of King Arthur and the Knights of the Round Table are to be heard in all corners of our realm. Bright! Beautiful! Glorious! This is what I want for my reign and my court."

Eleanor kissed her son, "Then have these, you shall, Richard! I shall help plan your coronation and, if you permit me, find you a proper wife who can preside over your court when you are engaged elsewhere – like perhaps the next Crusade? I know you wish to answer the Pope's call to go to Jerusalem."

"You understand my heart before I speak it!" laughed Richard gratefully.

"Consider it done then! You shall have the greatest and most glorious coronation in the history of England and the best and most suitable of women for your queen!"

Eleanor of Aquitaine

Eleanor was true to her word. On the 3rd of September, 1189 in Westminster Abbey, the Archbishop of Canterbury anointed Richard as king of England in the most lavish coronation ceremony ever performed in England up to that time. For the first time since William II Rufus succeeded his father William I of Normandy, a son was crowned after his father as king. It was a glorious and peaceful continuation of royal dynastic power that after many years of war, civil war, and brutal totalitarianism. A time of celebration in England. All of it Eleanor's design. Her moment of glory as much as Richard's.

In London the city celebrated their new king with violence. Rumours flew through the city that Richard's first command was for all the Jews in London to be murdered and their homes destroyed. As Richard returned to court to feast with his noblemen and elite clergy, Londoners set about to do the king's bidding much as Reginald FitzUrse, William de Tracy, Hugh de Morville, and Richard le Bret had sought to do King Henry II's bidding when they murdered Thomas Becket. By first light, not a single London Jew still lived, nor home remained with one stone upon another. Among the martyred dead lay Jacob d'Orléans, one of the greatest Jewish scholars and philosophers of his time, particularly in matters of Jewish-Gentile laws.

It was a prelude to Richard's own violence against the Jews during the Third Crusade.

In the aftermath of the London massacres Eleanor set about the next great task for Richard's reign: finding him a suitable queen. For Richard, the perfect bride was the one with the largest dowry. Wars cost money. Richard could not get enough money, not if he was to fulfil his dreams of conquering and ruling all of the Holy Land. To this end Richard was willing to sell off lands, royal treasures, anything he could get his hands on.

"Your Highness are you certain it is wise for you to travel?" asked King Richard's chamberlain.

"Why shouldn't I travel" asked Eleanor as she selected another bliaut and laid it on her bed.

"If you must travel, why not stay in Normandy —or perhaps go home to Aquitaine? Why must you go all the way to Navarre where we cannot protect you?" pleaded the chamberlain.

Eleanor of Aquitaine

"King Sancho Garcés of Navarre is not going to negotiate with just anyone, not on a matter so important as his daughter Berengaria's hand in marriage. No. I must go myself and see to it that Richard's queen is suitable for him in temperament while ensuring the terms of the marriage benefit England and the king's needs politically and financially. Of all people I know Richard the best. I am the right person to go!"

The journey to King Sancho Garcés' court in Pampiona took over two weeks. Crossing the Pyrenees Eleanor, now sixty-nine years old, found the Navarre climate similar to that of Aquitaine. Reaching the town she found it a lovely if not exotic mix of architecture, cultures and languages. The smell of exotic foods from the Moorish south filled the air to blend with Basque, Castilian, and Aragonese flavours. As a lover of both travel and the finer creature comforts, Eleanor found her first impression of Garcés' city most pleasing.

"Bienvenue à Pampiona, Votre Altesse," greeted King Sancho in French as Eleanor navigated his crowded court.

"Oso pozik nago hemen egoteaz!" replied Eleanor in Basque.

Smiling the king embraced Eleanor, "How was your journey here?"

"Delightful," grinned Eleanor. "A bit different crossing the Pyrenees at my age than it was when I crossed them with King Louis le Jeune on our way to Antioch. My bones mind the mountain passes more than they did back then."

King Sancho guided Eleanor around the hall towards a quieter and more private room where they could talk, "Hard to believe he's been dead almost ten years now. How time flies! You, my lady are a survivor!"

"Sometimes it doesn't feel like it. These last few years have been hard. Henry's prisons, while comfortable, were still prisons."

"Fortunately you are free of all that!" affirmed Sancho.

Eleanor of Aquitaine

"Hence my coming to you now. The throne of England has passed to my third son Richard, a young man who prefers killing Jews and Saracens in the Holy Land over the demands of governing. He needs a queen, a woman capable of not only performing the ceremonial duties required of a consort, but also someone able to help manage the massive bureaucracy of our realms."

"Your youngest son John is not capable of handling the day to day administration on his brother's behalf?"

Eleanor parsed her words carefully, "John is … capable, yes. But he is also a bit high strung at times. Maybe justly so given his father's constant political intrigues. He doesn't trust easily and too often sees conspiracies around him that do not exist."

"You don't trust him," observed Sancho.

"Not completely, no. His distrust of pretty much everyone might make him a competent administrator of the day to day affairs of State, but it is not endearing."

King Sancho met her eyes, "You want an alternative to John's rule."

"Yes, I do. My father groomed me to rule Aquitaine. I need a wife for Richard who can rule England in his absence when required. I am told by your ambassadors that your daughter Berengaria might be just the person England needs."

"Berengaria is a fine lady. She is more than capable of fulfilling the ceremonial duties of your royal courts. As for ruling herself in times of need? That judgement I must defer to Your Highness. I think if you were to ask her you would find her most open minded to your designs for Richard's reign and perhaps an able ally in promoting the best interests of your peoples. Certainly she navigates the complexity of Pampiona well enough. You know of course that her mother was Sancha of Castile."

"Yes! I have heard that – and that King Sancho Garcés III perhaps unwisely divided Navarre among his three sons upon his death, creating the kingdoms of Castile and Aragon in the process. Your wife is a princess because of what seems to me an error in judgement."

"Navarre has suffered greatly since then, losing our kingdom in turn to Aragonese rule until my father restored Navarrese independence just over thirty six years ago. Trust me, dear Lady, a day does not pass in Navarre when we are not keenly aware of that legacy. Your son needs a queen for England. We need

Eleanor of Aquitaine

Aquitaine's help in remaining independent. To keep Navarre independent I am willing to offer my daughter —and a sizeable dowry if that will make her more attractive to him," offered King Sancho.

"When can I meet her?" asked Eleanor.

"Tonight, at dinner if you feel you will be washed and refreshed from your journey by then," suggested the king.

"I look forward to it!" smiled Eleanor.

Dinner at King Sancho's court sparkled and shined like gold. Determined to make a good impression on the former queen, King Sancho ordered his chefs to prepare the finest foods Navarre had to offer. From pintxo appetizers made with Idiazábal cheese and on fresh baked bread to garlic prawns, Navarrese beef, and lamb, the king treated Eleanor to the best of Basque cuisine. Local wines flowed freely to add to what he hoped was a persuasive array of culinary finery. Tray after tray of exquisitely prepared food flowed from the kitchen. Following a pre-prepared signal Berengaria floated into the banqueting hall, her pale saffron-coloured bliaut almost dancing across her petite body as she moved. A loosely woven veil made of soft Navarrese wool covered her dark brown hair. Dark brown eyes beamed her desire to please her potential mother-in-law.

Reaching the high table, Berengaria curtsied before Eleanor, "Bonsoir, Votre Altesse. Je suis Berengaria, princesse de Navarre."

"Je suis heureuse de vous rencontrer," replied Eleanor. "I have heard nothing but praise of you from your father since I arrived."

Berengaria sat down next to Eleanor and took a sip of wine, "You are from Aquitaine, our neighbour to the north?"

"I am. I was duchess of Aquitaine until the title passed to my son Richard. He is now king of England, duke of Aquitaine, Normandy, and Gascony, and count of Anjou and Maine. That means that if you should marry him you will be a queen, duchess, and countess all at the same time. Assuming Richard doesn't do something stupid and lose our lands to King Philippe Auguste," hinted Eleanor.

"What sort of man is he?" asked Berengaria.

"Adventurous—is that the word I want? Perhaps. He's a good knight, a leader of men in battle. A born warrior who loves music and poetry. My influence, perhaps. He was the only one of my sons to grow up with me in my court in Poitiers. You probably heard that his father King Henry and me did not get along very well …."

Berengaria laughed, "I think the whole of Christendom knows that King Henry kept you under house arrest for many years. I do hope Richard is kinder than his father was towards you."

"Richard's first act upon learning of his father's death was to release me from captivity. As a son he's a good man."

"Well then I hope he makes just as good a husband," laughed Berengaria.

"I think so—if you don't mind that he loves to be on campaign and fighting in the Holy Land rather than sitting in an office in London governing his people. If you accept him and this proposed marriage alliance becomes a reality it is very likely that a sometimes the task of governing will fall to you. Are you up for that?" queried Eleanor, the lightness of her voice concealing her genuine and extremely serious concerns on the matter.

Berengaria nodded, "I have helped my father govern since my mother's death a few years ago. I see no reason why I cannot govern England and its Plantagenet empire during times of the king's absence. Where I am not suited to make the decisions asked of me, I shall defer to you, if that is acceptable?"

"More than acceptable," agreed Eleanor.

"Very well then, I shall defer this matter to my father. If he decides this would be a good alliance for both England and Navarre then I would be happy to marry your Richard," consented Berengaria amicably.

Eleanor returned to Poitiers. Reporting to King Richard that Berengaria was a suitable bride, she set in motion the formal betrothal between the two. A year later she departed once more for Navarre, collecting Richard's bride from a different ship than King Richard. Meeting in Cyprus Richard married Berengaria in a lavish wedding ceremony held in the town of Limassol. While there he had her crowned queen of England before setting off himself to engage the Saracens in the Holy Land.

Eleanor of Aquitaine

"Did you hear the news, John?" asked Eleanor as she entered the king's privy chamber in the Tower of London. Half-drunk John Lackland sat on his brother's throne, mulling over reports and double checking the math in the ledgers in front of him – the job of King Richard's Exchequer, not his regents or chancellors.

John looked up at his mother, "What news?"

"Your brother the king has been moved to Mainz and is now under the power of Kaiser Heinrich VI who insists the king will remain in his empire until his ransom is paid."

"Let him rot there," declared John flippantly.

"You care nothing for your own brother?" asked Eleanor.

"Why should I?" growled John. "What has Richard ever done but deny me what I am due? He's a menace, worshipped for his bravery in battle yet he cannot be bothered to come to London to actually rule his people. England and our lands across the Channel are nothing more than a source of money to him to finance his pet military ventures in the Holy Land. He does not rule the power and does not attend to the affairs of state."

"I cannot argue with you about Richard's lack of concern for governing. He neglects our peoples just as badly as he neglects his beautiful wife," affirmed Eleanor.

"Lucky for me his choice of chancellors and justiciars are as poor as his administrative style: completely incompetent. Face it, Mother, whether you like it or not I am best suited at ruling England than anyone appointed by Richard."

"What about the queen?"

"Berengaria has never set foot in England. She's Navarrese. She doesn't know the English people as I do, though I grant if she wishes to help govern our duchies and counties across the channel, she is welcome to do so. Give her something to do anyway since Richard doesn't seem interested in being a proper husband."

"I would not criticize Richard too heavily when it comes to his marriage," chided Eleanor. "You are notoriously unfaithful towards your wife, the countess of Gloucester. That you cheat on her with married women has estranged you from noblemen and commoners alike. I wouldn't be surprised at all if she demanded an annulment from the pope, much as I demanded my divorce from Louis."

"What Isabella wants or does not want is none of my concern," yelled John hotly. Grabbing his silver chalice he flung it across the room, spilling wine everywhere.

Eleanor of Aquitaine

Eleanor eyed her youngest son, "The Kaiser will demand a ransom for your brother. I intend to help Berengaria raise it. The revenue from royal lands is inadequate now that Richard has sold so many of them off to finance his crusade. We will have to find other means to raise the money."

"The Church has plenty of money – both lands and precious things made of gold, silver, and usually encrusted with jewels. Start there. If you insist on getting my 'dear brother' back from the Kaiser's prison then I suppose I can offer some of the money I get from men and noblemen willing to pay to avoid military service. Will that satisfy you, Mother?"

"It's a start, John, thank you!" acknowledged Eleanor with a slight bow.

"Now, Mother, if you don't mind – I really need to go over these numbers again. If we have to raise funds to free my brother then we can hardly afford to let the sheriffs and clergy cheat us out of what they owe in taxes and other fees."

Eleanor sighed, "Very well then, I shall leave you to it. Berengaria and I will work together on collecting the monies for Richard ourselves. But please, my dear boy, stop aggravating people, if you can? Much more is to be gained by being nice to people than agitating them …."

Eleanor and Berengaria successfully raised the ransom for King Richard, a staggering sum of 150,000 marks that was more than triple the annual income for the English crown at the time. In February 1194, Eleanor retrieved Richard from Mainz and tried to persuade him to return to England and govern his people. Like his father Henry, Richard remained obstinate and returned to war, this time against King Philippe Auguste of France. In late March, 1199 while laying siege to castle Châlus-Chabrol in Aquitaine a boy struck Richard with a crossbow quarrel. He died there after several days, his beloved mother Eleanor with him for his final hours.

Youngest son John Lackland ascended the English throne, taking a new wife, also named Isabella, after Isabella of Gloucester secured her annulment from him. Together John and Isabella of Angoulême had five children, despite John's continued infidelities and persistent agitations. In 1215 John's agitations towards his clergy and nobility culminated in the Great Charter – the Magna Carta – John's most enduring legacy.

Eleanor of Aquitaine

For Eleanor's part she spent the remaining years of her life in retirement in Anjou, cared for by the nuns at Fonteyrault Abbey near Chinon. In 1204 she died and was buried there at the abbey. She was eighty-two years old.

Laurel A. Rockefeller
Medieval Time

The medieval day was not divided up the same as we do today. Though there were twenty four hours in a day, the hours recognized by the church were not even in amount and were largely based on the amount of daylight received.

Until the 12th century, there were six hours recognized in the day. Of these, three of them were hold overs from the Roman Empire. Originally terce, sext, and none were the designated times Romans used to change the guards at their posts. When the Roman Empire ceased to govern northern Europe, the Church decided that these watch-post change times were well suited for prayers and therefore made terce, sext, and none part of the liturgical day.

<u>The hours were:</u>

Matins: first light, roughly an hour before sunrise.

Prime: not added until the 12th century, prime continued the daybreak prayers from matins following an hour to two hour break for personal hygiene and breakfast.

Terce: the third hour of the day, roughly 9 am.

Sext: the sixth hour of the day, roughly at noon.

Eleanor of Aquitaine

None: the ninth hour from dawn.

Vespers: the sixth of the seven ecclesiastical hours, vespers prayers are offered in the mid to late afternoon and always before sunset. The name is derived from the planet Venus, the "evening star."

Compline: the final ecclesiastical hour in a day. Compline prayers are prayed after sunset and the evening meal.

Example: on 22nd December 1065 in London, the liturgical hours corresponded to:

Matins: 6:40 am

(Sunrise: 8:07 am)

Terce: 9:40 am

Sext: 12:20 pm

None: 1:40 pm

Vespers: 3:00 pm

(Sunset: 3:58 pm)

Compline: 5:00 - 6:00 pm

Laurel A. Rockefeller

As you can see, prime was not part of the canonical hours when Westminster Abbey was dedicated. By contrast, Christmas 1125 (Empress Matilda's first Christmas in London following the death of Kaiser Heinrich V in May) experienced prime as part of her day:

Matins: 6:40 am

Prime: 8:00 am

(Sunrise): 8:07am

Terce: 9:40 am

Sext: 12:20 pm

None: 1:40 pm

Vespers: 3:00 pm

(Sunset: 3:58 pm)

Compline: 5:00 - 6:00 pm

In the 13th century, the English moved None to midday, perhaps to facilitate an increasingly numerous merchant and artisan class. This move did not spread to the continent until the 14th century.

Eleanor of Aquitaine

The Hours in London on Christmas day during the reign of King Henry III Plantagenet (reigned 1216 – 1272):

Matins: 6:40 am

Prime: 8:00 am

Terce: 9:20 am

Sext: 11:00 am

None: 12:20 pm

Vespers: 3:00 pm

Compline: 5-6 pm

See http://www.troynovant.com/Farrell-A/Essays/Medieval-Timekeeping.html and https://andreacefalo.com/2014/01/29/telling-time-in-the-middle-ages-5-things-you-didnt-know/

Laurel A. Rockefeller
König Verses Kaiser

German rulers could control Germany alone or rule a larger realm known in English as the "Empire of the Romans" or, starting in the late Renaissance, "Holy Roman Empire." In Latin the empire is called "Sacrum Romanum Imperium."

When ruling Germany alone, their title was "römisch-deutscher König." "König" for short.

When ruling as Emperor of the Romans, their title was "Kaiser des römisch-deutschen Reiches" or simply "Kaiser." In Latin, the Kaisers were called "Imperator Romanorum."

Unlike other countries, German rulers typically needed papal endorsement and a papal coronation in order to assume full power. Without such, they could rule in Germany — but only in Germany and not the larger Empire. During the Salian (1027-1125) dynasty conflicts with the popes often resulted in the pope refusing to crown the German kings as Kaisers, even when in practice he ruled over the whole of the empire. In the case of Heinrich V, Pope Paschal II refused to crown his new queen, Matilda as Kaiserin (Imperatrix

Eleanor of Aquitaine

Romanorum). Instead, she was crowned Kaiserin by Archbishop Bourdin of Portugal in 1117.

In the 11th and 12th centuries, the Empire mostly consisted of the kingdom of Germany, kingdom of Italy, Burgundy, and Bohemia.

The Empire would continue to expand and contract across the centuries until its final dissolution in 1806 during the Napoleonic Wars.

Laurel A. Rockefeller
Timeline

583; Gallo-Roman Desiderius of Aquitaine is gifted the duchy of Aquitaine by Merovingian king of the Franks, Chilperic I. Beginning of Aquitaine as an independent duchy.

987; Hugh Capet establishes the Capetian dynasty, ending Carolingian rule of France. Capet's rule extends only to Paris and its suburbs.

1029; King Sancho Garcés III of Pampiona (Navarre) annexes the county of Castile into Navarre.

1035; death of King Sancho Garcés III. Navarre is divided among his three sons, creating three kingdoms (Navarre, Castile, and Aragon) out of Navarre.

1070, 22nd October; birth of William IX The Troubadour, duke of Aquitaine.

1081, 1st December; birth of Louis le Gros in Paris.

1098, May; Kaiser Heinrich IV has son Heinrich crowned as Kaiser Heinrich V on condition that the son never seek to rule over his father. The arrangement lasts for only six years.

1099; birth of William X to Duke William IX of Aquitaine.

1100 5th August; coronation of Prince Henry as King Henry I of England.

Eleanor of Aquitaine

1100 11th November; King Henry I of England marries Princess Edith of Scotland who takes the name "Matilda" when she is crowned queen of England.

1102 7th February; Matilda of Scotland gives birth to Princess Matilda in Sutton Courtenay in Oxfordshire.

1103; birth of Aénor de Châtellerault in northern Poitou near Poitiers.

1103 5th August; Queen Matilda of Scotland gives birth to King Henry's only legitimate son, Prince William Ætheling.

1105; birth of Raimond de Poitiers to Duke William IX of Aquitaine.

1113 24th August; birth of Geoffrey Plantagenet to Count Fulk V of Anjou and Eremburga de La Flèche, Countess of Maine and Lady of Château-du-Loir.

1114 7th January; Princess Matilda weds Holy Roman Emperor Heinrich V in Saint Martin's Cathedral in Mainz.

1115 3rd August; Adelaide of Maurienne marries King Louis VI in Paris.

1117 Archbishop Bourdin crowns Matilda Empress of the Romans in Rome. Matilda begins to use the title "Imperatrix" (empress).

1120; birth of Prince Louis le Jeune to King Louis VI and Queen Adelaide of Maurienne.

Laurel A. Rockefeller

1120 25th November; Empress Matilda's brother William Ætheling perishes in the Wreck of the White Ship leaving Matilda as Henry I's only surviving legitimate child and natural heir.

1121; Aénor de Châtellerault weds Duke William X of Aquitaine.

1122; Aénor de Châtellerault gives birth to her daughter Aliénor (Eleanor) in Aquitaine.

1125; Aénor de Châtellerault gives birth to her second daughter Petronilla.

1125 23 May; Emperor Heinrich V dies in Utrecht, Friesland in the Netherlands. Soon after King Henry I recalls Empress Matilda to his court in England.

1127 Henry I names Matilda as his heir with promises by his barons to support her inheritance.

1127 April; in obedience to her father King Henry I, Empress Matilda agrees to marry Geoffrey Plantagenet of Anjou and Maine.

1128 17th June; Matilda weds Geoffrey Plantagenet of Anjou in Le Mans in Maine.

1130; death of Eleanor's mother Duchess Aénor de Châtellerault in Talmont, Aquitaine.

1131, 25th October; following the death of his elder brother Phillip, Louis le Jeune is crowned co-king of France in Reims Cathedral.

Eleanor of Aquitaine

1131 8th September; magnates attending council in Northampton renew their homage to Empress Matilda and officially recognize her as King Henry's heir. Matilda agrees to return to her marriage soon after.

1131 King Henry of England takes Empress Matilda back to London at the protest of her estranged husband Geoffrey of Anjou.

1132, 21st April; birth of King Sancho Garcés VI of Pampiona.

1133 5th March; Empress Matilda gives birth to her son Prince Henry, the future King Henry II in the city of Le Mans in Anjou.

1134 1st June; Empress Matilda gives birth to her second son, Geoffrey, Count of Nantes.

1135 1st December; King Henry I dies.

1135 26th December; coronation King Stephen at Westminster Abbey. Beginning of the civil war known as the "Anarchy."

1136 22nd July; Empress Matilda gives birth to William Fitzempress at her château in Argentan, Normandy.

1137 March; Duke X of Aquitaine leaves Eleanor and sister Petronilla in Bordeaux under the protection of its archbishop before continuing on his pilgrimage to Santiago de Compostela.

Laurel A. Rockefeller

1137 9th April; death of Eleanor's father, Duke William X of dysentery while on pilgrimage to Santiago de Compostela in Galicia, Spain. Eleanor becomes Duchess of Aquitaine. King Louis VI le Gros becomes guardian over both Eleanor and her inheritance.

1137, July; Eleanor of Aquitaine marries Prince Louis le Jeune of France in the Cathédrale-Primatiale Saint-André de Bordeaux.

1137, 1st August; death King Louis VI le Gros.

1137 25th December. Coronation of King Louis VII le Jeune and Queen Eleanor.

1138 King David I of Scotland invades England three times in support of his niece Matilda. On 22nd of August King Stephen's forces defeat him at the Battle of the Standard near North Allerton, Yorkshire.

1139 Dowager queen Adelheid van Leuven receives her stepdaughter Matilda at her home at Arundel Castle in Sussex, enabling Matilda to pursue the crown of England directly. Marriage of Adelheid van Leuven to William d'Albini.

1141; King Stephen is captured at the Battle of Lincoln by Matilda's half-brother Robert Fitzroy, Earl of Gloucester. Matilda imprisons Stephen in Bristol.

1142; King Stephen of England imprisons Empress Matilda in Oxford Castle. Cunningly she dresses in white and escapes in a snow storm.

Eleanor of Aquitaine

1145; Henry Plantagenet meets Thomas Becket; start of their friendship.

1145, April; Eleanor gives birth to her eldest daughter, Marie de France.

1145; Pope Eugenius III issues a formal Crusade bull, "Quantum praedecessores" ("How Much Our Predecessors") calling for a second crusade.

1145, Autumn; Pope Eugenius III asks King Louis VII le Jeune to led a second crusade.

1145, 25th December; Louis VII le Jeune declares intention to join Second Crusade. Inspired by Bernard de Clairvaux' passionate sermons promoting the crusade, Eleanor declares she will join the crusade as well, leading any from Aquitaine who will join her.

1147 death of Robert Fitzroy, Earl of Gloucester. Empress Matilda retires to her estates in France.

1147 May; Kaiser Conrad III departs for Constantinople, arriving in September.

1147 June; Louis VII and Eleanor depart for Constantinople with Eleanor leading forces from Aquitaine.

1147 October; Louis VII and Eleanor arrive at Constantinople.

1147 24th October; Konrad III's crusaders are destroyed in Anatolia. Konrad barely escapes with his life.

1147, November; Konrad III meets with Louis VII and Eleanor in Ephesus. Konrad becomes ill and returns to Constantinople.

1148, 28th July; an ill-conceived plan to take Damascus leads to a crushing defeat for Louis VII, Eleanor, and the other Christians. Louis and Eleanor board separate ships for home.

1149, May; pirates attack Louis and Eleanor's ships. Weather forces Eleanor's ship south of the Barbary Coast.

1149, June; Raimond de Poitiers is captured during the Battle of Inab and beheaded by Shirkuh, uncle of Saladin.

1149, mid-July; arriving in Palermo Sicily, Eleanor learns that both she and Louis have been presumed dead. Roger of Sicily reunites Eleanor with Louis. Eleanor and Louis set off to meet Pope Eugenius III in Tusculum. Pope refuses Eleanor's request for a divorce and reconciles the couple. Eleanor becomes pregnant for a second time.

1150; Eleanor give birth to her second daughter by King Louis VII, Alix de France. Sancho Garcés VI of Pampiona drops the title "king of Pampiona" in favour of "king of Navarre."

1151 7th September; death of Geoffrey Plantagenet. Henry Plantagenet becomes Duke of Normandy and Count of Anjou and Maine.

Eleanor of Aquitaine

1152, 12th March; King Louis VII le Jeune and Eleanor of Aquitaine and four archbishops assemble at Castle Beaugency to dissolve the marriage. Eleanor granted an annulment of their marriage on grounds of cosangularity. Custody of their daughters Marie and Alix is given to King Louis.

1152, 18th May; Eleanor weds Henry Plantagenet at the Cathédrale-Primatiale Saint-André de Bordeaux and becomes daughter in law to Empress Matilda of England.

1153, 24th May; death of King David I of Scotland. David's grandson Malcolm ascends the Scottish throne as King Malcolm IV.

1153 17th August; Eleanor gives birth to her first son by King Henry, William. The infant is immediately given the title "Count of Poitiers," one of the lesser titles Eleanor inherited from her father.

1153 December; The Treaty of Westminster ends The Anarchy. Signed by King Stephen and Matilda's son Henry Plantagenet, the document ending the war between Stephen and Matilda makes no mention of her.

1154; Thomas Becket accepts the office of Chancellor from Henry II.

Laurel A. Rockefeller

1154 25th October; King Stephen de Blois dies in Dover. In compliance with the Treaty of Westminster, Henry Plantagenet succeeds Stephen as king of England. Eleanor's inherited lands, including Aquitaine, become property of King Henry II and under English control therein. The Aquitaine city of Bordeaux remains English until 1453.

1154 18th November; death of Adelaide of Maurienne.

1154 19th December; Coronation of King Henry II and Queen Eleanor.

1155; 28th February. Eleanor gives birth to son Henry, also known as Henry the Young King. King Henry II elevates William d'Albini to "Earl of Arundel."

1156; Eleanor gives birth to King Henry II's eldest daughter, Princess Matilda.

1156, 2nd April; death of William IX, Count of Poitiers, at the age of 2 ½.

1157; Eleanor gives birth to Prince Richard, the future King Richard I. Death of Empress Matilda's half-brother (by Princess Nest ferch Rhys of Deheubarth) Henry Fitzhenry in Ynys Môn, Gwynedd.

1158 26th July; death of Empress Matilda's son Geoffrey, Count of Nantes.

1158, August; Henry II moves to Normandy.

1158, 23rd September; Eleanor gives birth to son Geoffrey.

Eleanor of Aquitaine

1159; Eldest daughter Marie de France marries Henri, Comte de Champagne and becomes known as "Marie de Champagne."

1161; birth of second daughter Eleanor of England.

1162 2nd June; Thomas Becket is ordained as a priest.

1162 3rd June; Thomas Becket is consecrated as the Archbishop of Canterbury. Within days Becket resigns his position as Chancellor.

1163, January; Henry II returns to London.

1164 30th January; death of Empress Matilda's youngest son William Fitzempress.

1164; Under pressure from King Henry II, Archbishop Thomas Becket orders his bishops to adopt the Constitutions of Clarendon defining the relationships between Canon (church-based) and secular (government-based) law.

1164, 2nd November; Becket arrives in Flanders. Initially he stays at the Abbey of St. Bertin near Clair-Marais.

1165; Queen Sancha of Castile gives birth to Princess Berengaria Sánchez of Navarre.

1165, October; Eleanor gives birth to daughter Joan of England.

1166, 12th June; Becket excommunicates several of Henry II's court favourites.

1166, 24th December; birth of son John Lackland.

1167; Eleanor and King Henry II separate. Eleanor moves to Poitiers. Sister Alix follows her into exile.

1167 10th September; Empress Matilda dies in Rouen.

1168; Prince Richard is made duke of Aquitaine.

1169, January; Henry II and Becket meet in Montmirail to try to resolve their conflicts. They part company sworn enemies.

1170, 14th July; Becket's enemy the Archbishop of York crowns Prince Henry as king of England to rule concurrently with his father.

1170, 27th July; Becket and Henry II meet again, this time in Freteval. Peace established between the king and Becket.

1170, 1st December; Becket returns to Canterbury.

1170 29th December; Murder of Thomas Becket.

1172; Prince Richard is made duke of Poitiers.

1173; Eleanor joins her sons Henry, Richard, Geoffrey, and John in an uprising against King Henry II. While her sons successfully rendezvous with King Louis VII to coordinate their battle plans, Eleanor is captured by King Henry II and imprisoned. Eleanor stays in prison until Henry's death.

1173, 21st February; Thomas Becket is canonized.

Eleanor of Aquitaine

1174, 8th July; Henry II returns to England after fighting his sons for control of his continental possessions.

1174, 12th July; Henry performs penance for his role in Thomas Becket's murder.

1174, 13th July; royal loyalists capture rebel leader William the Lion and his supporters. End of Rebellion against Henry II in England.

1174, 30th September; Henry II's sons renew fealty to King Henry II in a ceremony in Normandy. End of Revolt of 1173-1174.

1180, 18th September; death of King Louis VII le Jeune. Philippe II Auguste becomes king of France, the first French king to call himself "king of France" instead of "king of the Franks."

1183, 11th June; death of Eleanor's second son, King Henry the Young King. Richard becomes heir to the English throne.

1186, 19th August; death of Eleanor's son Geoffrey II, duke of Brittany.

1189; John Lackland marries Isabella, countess of Gloucester.

1189; death of Eleanor's daughter Matilda. Beginning of Third Crusade.

1189 6th July; death of King Henry II.

Laurel A. Rockefeller

1189 3rd September; coronation of King Richard the Lionheart. Eleanor begins searching for a proper queen consort for Richard, eventually choosing Spanish Princess Berengaria Sánchez of Navarre for him.

1190; death of sister Petronilla while on board a ship back to France.

1191 12th May; King Richard Coeur de Lion weds Berengaria of Navarre in Limassol, Cyprus. Soon after Richard has Berengaria crowned as queen of England.

1191, June; Richard arrives in the Holy Land.

1191, July; King Richard restores Acre to Christian control.

1192; The Third Crusade ends in a stalemate and treaty signed between King Richard and Saladin.

1192, 20th December; King Leopold V of Austria captures King Richard in Italy.

1193, February; King Leopold V delivers King Richard to Kaiser Heinrich VI.

1194, 4th February; Richard Coeur de Lion released from captivity in Mainz after Eleanor of Aquitaine and Queen Berengaria pay his ransom of 150, 000 marks (equivalent to approximately 3.3 billion USD in 2022).

1199; Marriage between John Lackland and Isabella of Gloucester is annulled. Fontevrault-l'Abbaye is founded.

Eleanor of Aquitaine

1199, 6th April; death King Richard I Lionheart.

1199, 27th May; John Lackland crowned king of England in Westminster Abbey.

1199, 4th September; death of Joan of England.

1200; King John marries Isabella of Angoulême.

1204; death of Eleanor of Aquitaine.

1209; excommunication of King John I Lackland.

1215, June; King John Lackland signs the Magna Carta.

1216, 19th October; death of King John I Lackland. Eldest son Henry of Winchester becomes King Henry III.

1230, 23rd December. Death of Queen Berengaria of Navarre, consort to King Richard Lionheart.

1328; the Capetian dynasty becomes House Valois. Beginning of Valois dynasty.

1453; France annexes Aquitaine. End of English rule over Aquitaine.

Laurel A. Rockefeller

Suggested Reading and Bibliography

Eleanor of Aquitaine (Aliénor d'Aquitaine)

History.com: Eleanor of Aquitaine

http://www.history.com/topics/british-history/eleanor-of-aquitaine

World History Encyclopaedia: Eleanor of Aquitaine

https://www.worldhistory.org/Eleanor_of_Aquitaine/

Eleanor of Aquitaine: queen consort of France and England

https://www.britannica.com/biography/Eleanor-of-Aquitaine

The descendants of Henry II and Eleanor of Aquitaine

http://historyofengland.typepad.com/.a/6a0147e0fd1b4a970b017744982c3b970d-pi

Eleanor of Aquitaine
Duke of Aquitaine

https://en-academic.com/dic.nsf/enwiki/118919

British Heritage: A history of Eleanor of Aquitaine

https://britishheritage.com/history/history-eleanor-aquitaine

Eleanor of Aquitaine marries Henry of Anjou

https://www.historytoday.com/archive/eleanor-aquitaine-marries-henry-anjou

Annulment of Eleanor of Aquitaine's Marriage

https://www.creativehistorian.co.uk/blog/read_125874/annulment-of-eleanor-of-aquitaines-marriage.html

English Heritage: Eleanor of Aquitaine

https://www.english-heritage.org.uk/learn/histories/women-in-history/eleanor-aquitaine/

Laurel A. Rockefeller

Capetian Dynasty

Louis VII de France (1120-1180)

https://familypedia.fandom.com/wiki/Louis_VII_de_France_(1120-1180)

WikiTree: Louis (Capet) de France (abt. 1120 - 1180)

https://www.wikitree.com/wiki/Capet-13

France, Kingdom of / Louis VII le Jeune (King Louis VII the Younger)

https://onlinecoin.club/Info/Reigns/France_Kingdom/King_Louis_VII/

Louis VI (The Fat) King of France

http://homepages.rpi.edu/~holmes/Hobbies/Genealogy2/ps07/ps07_332.htm

Capetian Dynasty

https://www.britannica.com/topic/Capetian-dynasty

Eleanor of Aquitaine

Valois Dynasty

https://www.britannica.com/topic/Valois-dynasty

House of Bourbon

https://www.britannica.com/topic/house-of-Bourbon

French Monarchs Family Tree

https://youtu.be/fPR9BFmPKdU

Merovingian Kings Family Tree

https://youtu.be/kjBRCuj9pCU

Plantagenet Dynasty

John Lackland

https://www.royal.uk/john-lackland

Laurel A. Rockefeller

Britannica: Richard I Lionheart

https://www.britannica.com/biography/Richard-I-king-of-England

BBC History: Richard I (1157 - 1199)

https://www.bbc.co.uk/history/historic_figures/richar
d_i_king.shtml

On this day in history - Richard the Lionheart was captured by Leopold V of Austria

https://www.historyscotland.com/history/on-this-day-in-history-richard-the-lionheart-was-captured-by-leopold/

How did Richard the Lionheart Die? And where is he buried?

https://www.historyextra.com/period/medieval/how-when-richard-lionheart-died/

Eleanor of Aquitaine's Children and Grandchildren

https://www.thoughtco.com/eleanor-of-aquitaines-children-and-grandchildren-3529605

Eleanor of Aquitaine

Royal Family History: King Henry II (1154-1189)

http://www.britroyals.com/kings.asp?id=henry2

The conflict between Henry II and Thomas a Becket

https://www.britainexpress.com/History/Thomas-a-Becket.htm

The Character and Legacy of Henry II

https://www.bbc.co.uk/history/british/middle_ages/henryii_character_01.shtml

The Revolt of 1173-74

https://military-history.fandom.com/wiki/Revolt_of_1173%E2%80%9374

The Coronation of Richard the Lionheart

https://www.angevinworld.com/blog/coronation-richard-lionheart/

Laurel A. Rockefeller

Berengaria of Navarre: Queen Consort to Richard I

https://www.thoughtco.com/berengaria-of-navarre-3529619

Berengaria of Navarre

https://www.englishmonarchs.co.uk/plantagenet_37.html

4 February 1194: Richard the Lionheart is ransomed

https://moneyweek.com/425142/4-february-1194-richard-the-lionheart-is-ransomed

Jacob of Orleans

https://www.encyclopedia.com/religion/encyclopedias-almanacs-transcripts-and-maps/jacob-orleans

King Henry II (documentary)

https://youtu.be/-ZHen6A_rrw (part one)

https://youtu.be/a6uXB7aaJeQ (part two)

https://youtu.be/TU4HG5skFCU (part three)

Eleanor of Aquitaine
<u>Thomas Becket</u>

Britannica: Thomas Becket

https://www.britannica.com/biography/Saint-Thomas-Becket

Becket: the Murder that Shook the Middle Ages

https://blog.britishmuseum.org/thomas-becket-the-murder-that-shook-the-middle-ages/

Becket, the Church, and Henry II

http://www.bbc.co.uk/history/british/middle_ages/becket_01.shtml

Thomas Becket: Murder in the Cathedral

https://www.historic-uk.com/HistoryUK/HistoryofEngland/Thomas-Becket/

The incredible life of Sir Thomas Becket and his gruesome murder

https://britishheritage.com/history/life-sir-thomas-becket-murder

Laurel A. Rockefeller
Empress Matilda of England

Medieval Life and Times: Empress Matilda

http://www.medieval-life-and-times.info/medieval-women/empress-matilda.htm

History Today: The Wedding of Princess Matilda

http://www.historytoday.com/richard-cavendish/wedding-princess-matilda

About Education: Timeline for the Empress Matilda

http://womenshistory.about.com/od/empressmatilda/a/matilda_timelin.htm

The Kings and Queens of England – Episode One Normans

https://youtu.be/0PfoYkgoBZQ

Historic UK: Empress Maud

http://www.historic-uk.com/HistoryUK/HistoryofEngland/Empress-Maud/

Eleanor of Aquitaine

Spartacus Educational: Queen Matilda

http://spartacus-educational.com/MEDmatilda.htm

English Monarchs: Geoffrey Plantagenet, Count of Anjou (1113-1151)

http://www.englishmonarchs.co.uk/plantagenet_42.html

Britannica: Robert, Earl of Gloucester

https://www.britannica.com/biography/Robert-Earl-of-Gloucester

King Stephen of England

Stephen of Blois

http://www.biography.com/people/stephen-of-blois-9493736

Laurel A. Rockefeller

The Royal Family History: King Stephen, 1135-1154

http://www.britroyals.com/kings.asp?id=stephen

The English Monarchs: King Stephen

http://www.englishmonarchs.co.uk/normans_4.htm

Seduced by History: King Stephen

http://seducedbyhistory.blogspot.com/2009/05/king-stephen-vs-empress-maud.html

King Stephen Biography

http://www.medieval-life-and-times.info/medieval-kings/king-stephen-biography.htm

Stephen and the Welsh

http://history-england-the-anarchy.blogspot.com/2011/01/addendum-stephen-and-welsh.html

Matilda of Boulogne

http://womenshistory.about.com/od/medbritishqueens/p/Matilda-of-Boulogne.htm

Eleanor of Aquitaine

Geni: Richard FitzGilbert, Lord of Clare

https://www.geni.com/people/Richard-FitzGilbert-Lord-of-Clare/6000000006125448136

Find a Grave: Richard Fitzgilbert de Clare

http://www.findagrave.com/cgi-bin/fg.cgi?page=gr&GRid=63613455

Norman Conquest & Angevin Dynasty

The Norman and Angevin/Plantagenet kings of England, 1066-1377

http://hoocher.com/Henry_II_of_England/Norman_Plantagenet_Kings.gif

The British Monarchy: The Normans

https://www.royal.gov.uk/HistoryoftheMonarchy/KingsandQueensofEngland/TheNormans/TheNormans.aspx

Laurel A. Rockefeller

The British Monarchy: The Angevins

https://www.royal.gov.uk/historyofthemonarchy/king
sandqueensofengland/theangevins/theangevins.aspx

Historic Royal Palaces: the Tower of London

http://www.hrp.org.uk/tower-of-london/

The Tower of London: the Chapel of St. John, White
Tower

http://www.englishmonarchs.co.uk/tower_london_17.
html

The British Monarchy: William the Conqueror

http://www.royal.gov.uk/historyofthemonarchy/kings
andqueensofengland/thenormans/williamitheconquero
r.aspx

BBC History: William II (Rufus)

http://www.bbc.co.uk/history/historic_figures/willia
m_ii_king.shtml

Eleanor of Aquitaine

Robert Fitzroy, the Earl of Gloucester

http://www.englishmonarchs.co.uk/normans_11.html

William Fitzgerald, Baron of Windsor and Pembroke

https://www.geni.com/people/William-FitzGerald/6000000004533176983

Adeliza of Louvain

http://www.newworldencyclopedia.org/entry/Adeliza_of_Louvain

William X, Duke of Aquitaine

https://www.britannica.com/biography/William-X

William X, Duke of Aquitaine

https://military-history.fandom.com/wiki/William_X,_Duke_of_Aquitaine

The Counts of Toulouse, the Dukes of Aquitaine and the Kings of England

https://www.midi-france.info/190202_aquitaine.htm

Laurel A. Rockefeller

Was the White Ship Disaster Mass Murder?

http://www.medievalists.net/2013/05/21/was-the-white-ship-disaster-mass-murder/

Henry I Beauclerc

http://www.englishmonarchs.co.uk/normans_3.htm

Arundel Castle

http://www.arundelcastle.org/

The Palace and the Normans

http://www.parliament.uk/about/living-heritage/building/palace/estatehistory/the-middle-ages/palace-normans/

History Today: The Harrying of the North

http://www.historytoday.com/james-aitcheson/harrying-north

Eleanor of Aquitaine

The Crusades

World History Encyclopaedia: The Second Crusade

https://www.worldhistory.org/Second_Crusade/

The Era of the Second and Third Crusades

https://www.britannica.com/event/Crusades/The-era-of-the-Second-and-Third-Crusades

The Fourth Crusade and the Latin empire of Constantinople

https://www.britannica.com/event/Crusades/The-Fourth-Crusade-and-the-Latin-empire-of-Constantinople

The Second Crusade – History of the Extraordinary 2nd Crusade

https://www.medievalchronicles.com/the-crusades/the-second-crusade/

Crusaders on the Baltic Shore – The Wendish Crusade (1147 – c.1185)

https://thepostgradchronicles.org/2017/07/09/crusaders-in-the-north-the-wendish-crusade-1147-c-1185/

Laurel A. Rockefeller

Crusader queens: the formidable female rulers of Jerusalem

https://www.historyextra.com/period/medieval/queens-crusades-women-rulers-who-jerusalem/

Christianity Today: Women of the Cross

https://www.christianitytoday.com/history/issues/issue-40/women-of-cross.html

Raymond, Prince of Antioch

https://www.britannica.com/biography/Raymond

Aquitaine and Its Neighbours

Britannica: Bordeaux

https://www.britannica.com/place/Bordeaux

Old Aquitaine, from the Dordogne to the Basque country

https://about-france.com/regions/aquitaine.htm

Eleanor of Aquitaine

How the Basques became an autonomous community within Spain

https://www.nationalgeographic.com/history/article/how-basques-became-autonomous-community-spain

Castile: Early History and Formation

https://www.spainthenandnow.com/spanish-history/early-christian-kingdoms-castile

European Kingdoms: Iberia - Castile

https://www.historyfiles.co.uk/KingListsEurope/IberiaCastile.htm

Kingdom of Navarre

https://www.britannica.com/place/Kingdom-of-Navarre

Fontevrault-l'Abbaye

https://www.britannica.com/place/Fontevrault-lAbbaye

Laurel A. Rockefeller

Music and Dance

Medieval Dance

http://www.medieval-life-and-times.info/medieval-life/medieval-dance.htm

Medieval Musical Instruments

https://www.medieval-life-and-times.info/medieval-music/medieval-musical-instruments.htm

Troubadours Medieval Musicians

https://www.medievalchronicles.com/medieval-music/medieval-musicians/troubadours-medieval-musicians/

The Hurdy Gurdy

https://youtu.be/gYJg9cLk1us

The Sound of the Rebec: Ja nun hons pris - Richard Leonhardt

https://youtu.be/XWA6oTr0vnU

Eleanor of Aquitaine

The Symphonia and Ordo Virtutum of Hildegard von Bingen

http://www.hildegard-society.org/p/music.html

Renaissance Instruments

http://www.educationscotland.gov.uk/learnlisteningon line/higherandadvancedhigher/musicaltopics/chamber music/instruments.asp

Sumer Is Icumen In

http://www.pteratunes.org.uk/Music/Music/Lyrics/su mmerisicumenin.html

Heart's Ease (Dance steps)

http://www.pbm.com/~lindahl/dance/Hearts_Ease.h tml

Hymns and Carols of Christmas: Drive the Cold Winter Away

http://www.hymnsandcarolsofchristmas.com/Hymns_ and_Carols/drive_the_cold_winter_away.htm

Laurel A. Rockefeller

What are Playford Dances?

https://round.soc.srcf.net/playford

Bransles

http://www.pbm.com/~lindahl/del/sections/bransles.html

Songs of and About Elizabethan Times

http://www.renfaire.com/Language/songs.html

Elizabethan Songs

http://www.elizabethan-era.org.uk/elizabethan-songs.htm

Greensleeves Lyrics

http://www.sixwives.info/greensleeves-lyrics.htm

Facsimile of John Playford's "The English Dancing Master"

http://www.pbm.com/~lindahl/playford_1651/

Eleanor of Aquitaine

William IX, Duke of Aquitaine Poems

https://mypoeticside.com/poets/william-ix-duke-of-aquitaine-poems

Food and Drink

Gode Cookery: Breakfast

http://www.godecookery.com/how2cook/howto05.htm

What's So Special About Bordeaux?

https://learn.winecoolerdirect.com/bordeaux-basics/

A Primer to Bordeaux Wine

https://winefolly.com/deep-dive/a-primer-to-bordeaux-wine/

Alcohol in the Middle Ages, Dark Ages, or Medieval Period

https://www.alcoholproblemsandsolutions.org/alcohol-in-the-middle-ages/

Laurel A. Rockefeller

Alcohol During the Renaissance: 15th & 16th Centuries

https://www.alcoholproblemsandsolutions.org/alcohol
-during-the-renaissance/

What is the Difference Between Beer and Ale?

https://www.delightedcooking.com/what-is-the-
difference-between-beer-and-ale.htm

Beer Cocktail Recipe | Chaucer's Braggot Cocktail IPA
Challenge

https://www.porchdrinking.com/articles/2018/05/29
/beer-cocktail-recipe-chaucers-braggot-cocktail-ipa-
challenge/

What's The Difference Between Mead, Cyser, Braggot
& Melomel?

https://www.vikingalchemist.com/mead-
blog/2020/1/28/whats-the-difference-between-mead-
cyser-braggot-amp-melomel

The Fascinating History of Crepes

https://www.ophdenver.com/the-fascinating-history-
of-crepes/

Eleanor of Aquitaine

10 foods from Navarra you should try in the Basque Country

https://www.paladarytomar.com/spain/10-foods-from-navarra/

Falconry and Aviculture

Falcons and Hawks Visit Notre Dame for Medieval Institute Tailgate

https://medieval.nd.edu/news-events/news/falcons-and-hawks-visit-campus/

All About Birds – Peregrine Falcon

https://www.allaboutbirds.org/guide/Peregrine_Falcon

Britannica: Peregrine Falcon

https://www.britannica.com/animal/peregrine-falcon

Laurel A. Rockefeller

Hawk Watch: Peregrine Falcon

https://hawkwatch.org/learn/factsheets/item/103-peregrine-falcon

Medieval Women: Hawking

https://rosaliegilbert.com/hawking.html

Hunting in France Around Bordeaux

http://www.gourmetfly.com/Huntmar.htm

France for Birdwatchers

https://about-france.com/wildlife/birds.htm

Bird Checklists of the World – Aquitaine

https://avibase.bsc-eoc.org/checklist.jsp?region=FRaq&list=howardmoore

All About Birds – Peregrine Falcon

https://www.allaboutbirds.org/guide/Peregrine_Falcon

Eleanor of Aquitaine

Roosters Crowing: Why, How Loud, When and More

https://www.chickensandmore.com/rooster-crowing/

Maps

The Angevin "Empire"

http://www.heritage-history.com/maps/philips/phil035.jpg

Henry III's territories

http://www.heritage-history.com/maps/gardiner/gard012.jpg

Medieval England and Wales

http://www.heritage-history.com/maps/philips/phil034.jpg

Wales and the Marches in the Thirteenth Century

http://www.heritage-history.com/maps/philips/phil036c.jpg

Laurel A. Rockefeller

Other resources

How to Drink Like a Norman

http://blog.english-heritage.org.uk/how-to-drink-like-a-norman/

English Coronation Oath

http://www.conservapedia.com/English_coronation_oath

Crowned King of England

http://historyoflaw.co.uk/crowned-king-of-england/

When Did the Catholic Church Decide Priests Should Be Celibate?
https://historynewsnetwork.org/article/696

7 French Christmas Traditions to Adopt

https://www.parisperfect.com/blog/2018/11/french-christmas-traditions/

Eleanor of Aquitaine
Money in the Middle Ages

https://machaut.weebly.com/money-in-the-middle-ages.html

Printed in Great Britain
by Amazon

20300330R00079